2ND EDITION

THE BIG BOOK OF JAZZ

PIANO · VOCAL · GUITAR

ISBN 0-793-51247-6

CORPORATION
7777 W. BLUEMOUND RD. P.O. BOX 13819 MILWAUKEE, WI 53213

Visit Hal Leonard Online at
www.halleonard.com

CONTENTS

4 All of You

8 All the Things You Are

12 Autumn Leaves

15 Basin Street Blues

18 Bess, You Is My Woman

26 Bewitched

30 The Birth of the Blues

35 Blues in the Night
(My Mama Done Tol' Me)

42 Call Me

47 Can't Help Lovin' Dat Man

50 Cherokee (Indian Love Song)

55 Darn That Dream

58 Days of Wine and Roses

61 Dearly Beloved

64 Easy to Love
(You'd Be So Easy to Love)

67 The End of a Love Affair

74 Falling in Love with Love

82 A Fine Romance

88 The Folks Who Live
on the Hill

96 The Girl from Ipanema
(Garôta de Ipanema)

93 God Bless' the Child

100 Harlem Nocturne

108 Have You Met Miss Jones?

110 Hello, Young Lovers

105 Honeysuckle Rose

116 How High the Moon

124 How Insensitive (Insensatez)

119 I Can't Get Started with You

128 I Could Write a Book

132 I Won't Dance

138 I'll Take Romance

142 I'm Beginning to See the Light

145 I've Got You Under My Skin

150 In a Mellow Tone

153 It Might As Well Be Spring

158 Jelly Roll Blues

166 Just in Time

169 La Fiesta

174 Lady Sings the Blues

177 The Last Time I Saw Paris

180 Long Ago (And Far Away)

183 Love Is Here to Stay

186 Lullaby of Birdland

190 Maiden Voyage

196 Maple Leaf Rag

193 Meditation (Meditacão)

202 My Favorite Things

206 My Funny Valentine

211 My One and Only Love

214 My Romance

218 A Night in Tunisia

224 A Nightingale Sang
     in Berkeley Square

234 Only Trust Your Heart

238 Ornithology

229 People Will Say We're in Love

240 Quiet Nights of Quiet Stars
     (Corcovado)

244 'Round Midnight

250 Route 66

255 Samba De Orfeu

258 Satin Doll

264 Skylark

261 Song for My Father

268 The Song Is You

272 (I Can Recall) Spain

279 Take the "A" Train

282 Tenderly

285 There Will Never Be
     Another You

288 This Masquerade

294 Waltz for Debby

297 The Way You Look Tonight

300 What Is This Thing
     Called Love?

305 What's New?

308 Yesterdays

310 You Are Too Beautiful

314 You Don't Know What Love Is

ALL OF YOU

from SILK STOCKINGS

Words and Music by
COLE PORTER

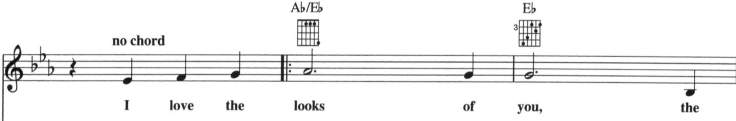

cer - tain love - ly lass, and it's

not a pass - ing fan - cy or a fan - cy pass. __

I love the looks of you, the

lure of you. I'd love to make a

ALL THE THINGS YOU ARE

from VERY WARM FOR MAY

Lyrics by OSCAR HAMMERSTEIN II
Music by JEROME KERN

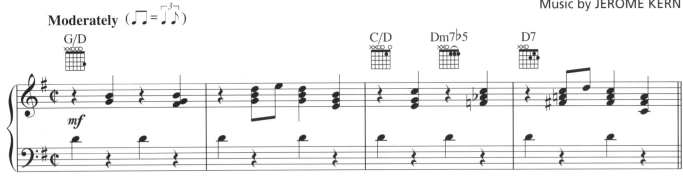

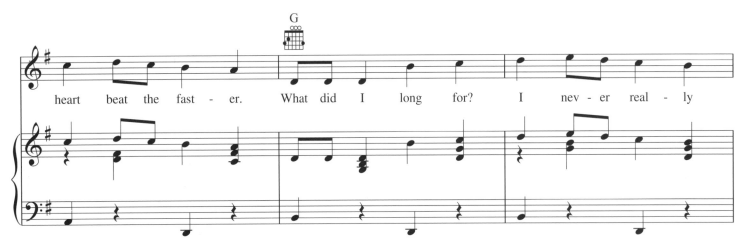

Time and a-gain I've longed for ad-ven-ture, some-thing to make my heart beat the fast-er. What did I long for? I nev-er real-ly knew. Find-ing your love, I've found my ad-ven-ture;

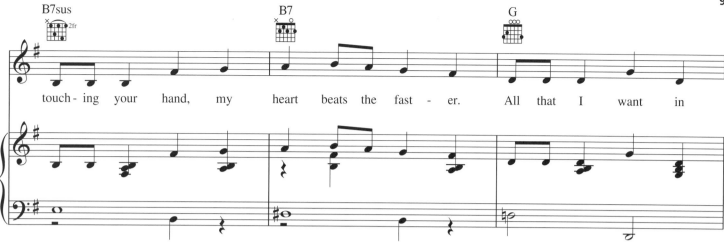

touch - ing your hand, my heart beats the fast - er. All that I want in

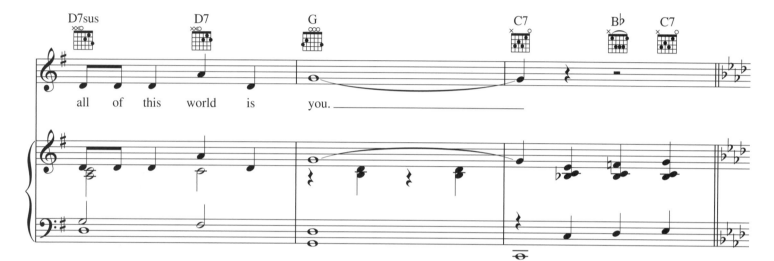

all of this world is you. _____

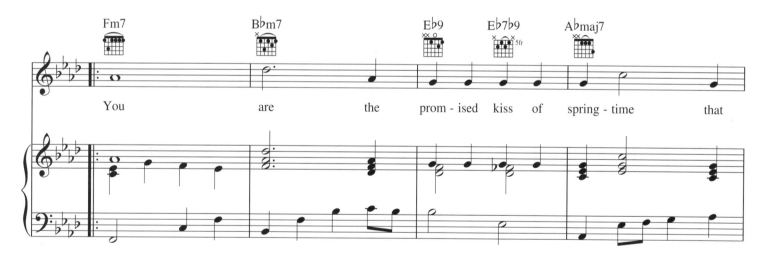

You are the prom - ised kiss of spring - time that

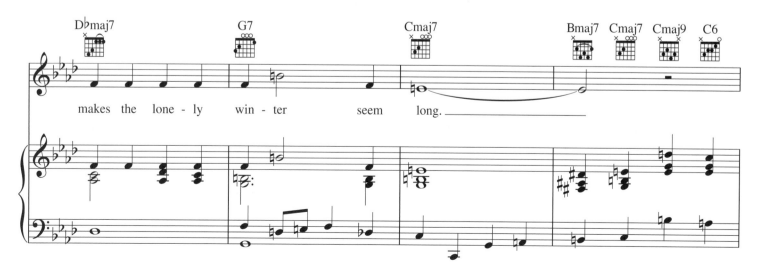

makes the lone - ly win - ter seem long. _____

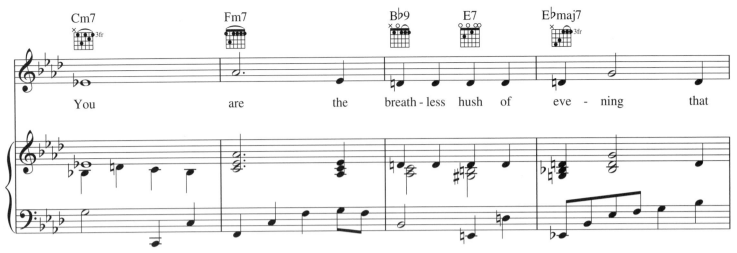

You are the breath-less hush of eve-ning that

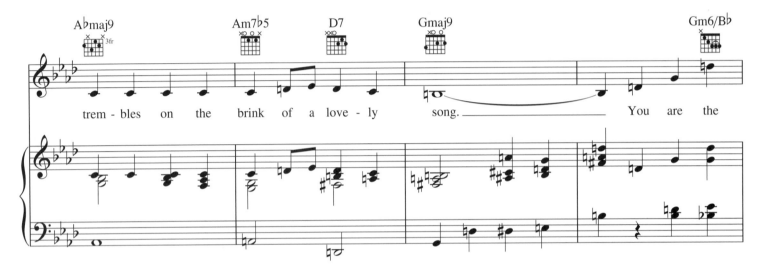

trem-bles on the brink of a love-ly song. _____ You are the

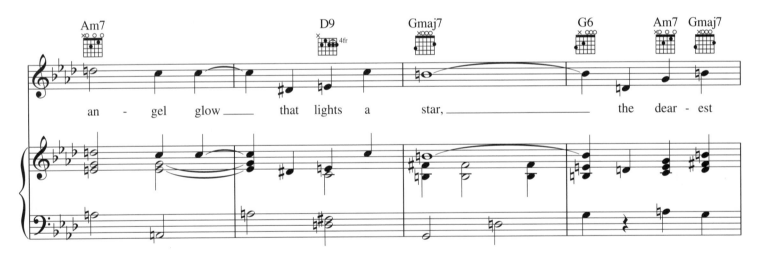

an - gel glow _____ that lights a star, _____ the dear-est

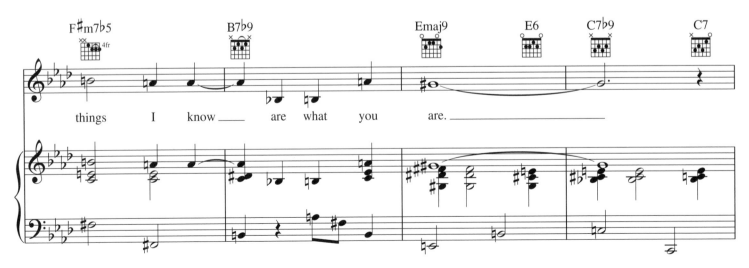

things I know _____ are what you are.

AUTUMN LEAVES

English lyric by JOHNNY MERCER
French lyric by JACQUES PREVERT
Music by JOSEPH KOSMA

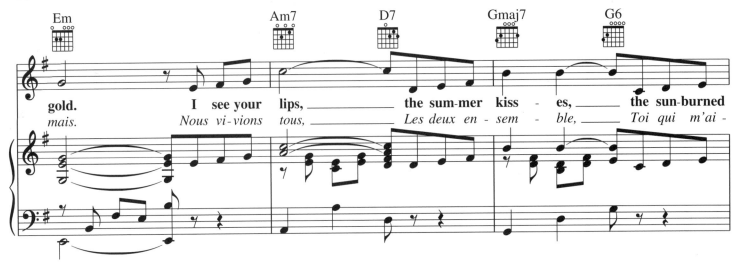

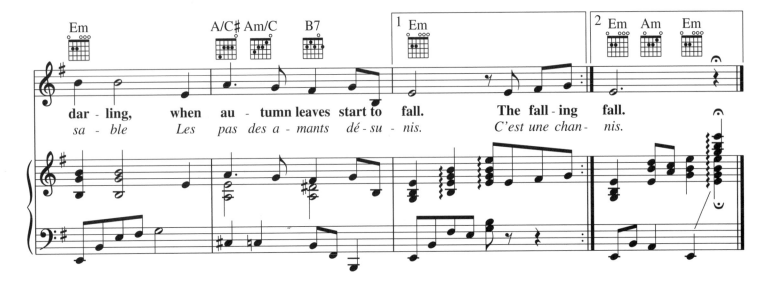

BASIN STREET BLUES

Words and Music by
SPENCER WILLIAMS

BESS, YOU IS MY WOMAN

from *PORGY AND BESS*

Words by IRA GERSHWIN and DUBOSE HEYWARD
Music by GEORGE GERSHWIN

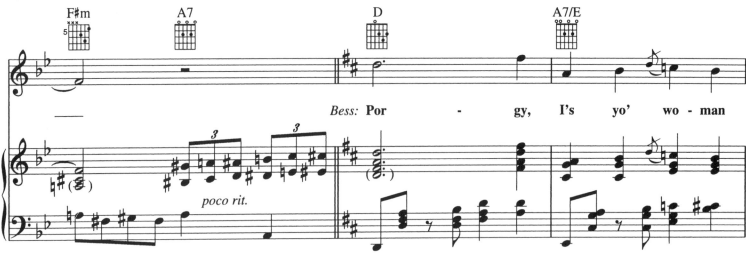

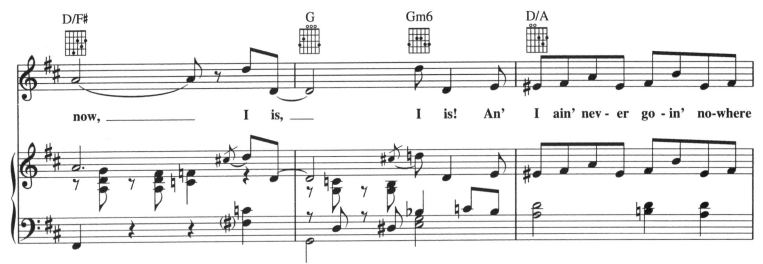

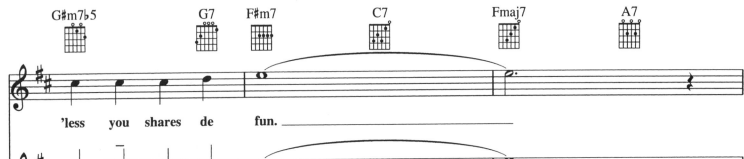

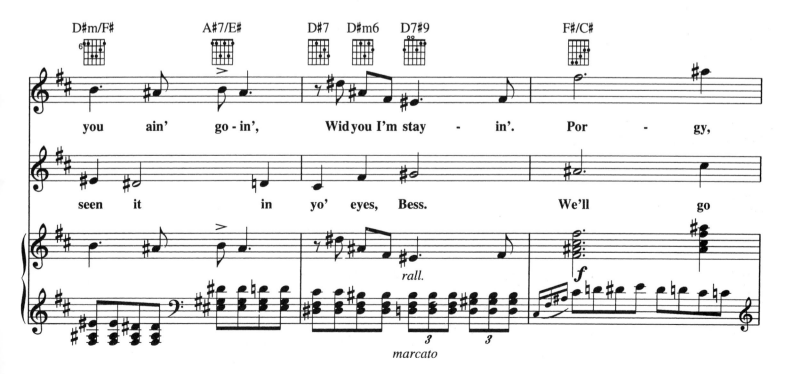

BEWITCHED
from PAL JOEY

Words by LORENZ HART
Music by RICHARD RODGERS

He's a fool and don't I know it, But a fool can have his charms;

I'm in love and don't I show it, Like a babe in arms.

Love's the same old sad sen-sa-tion, Late-ly I've not slept a wink,

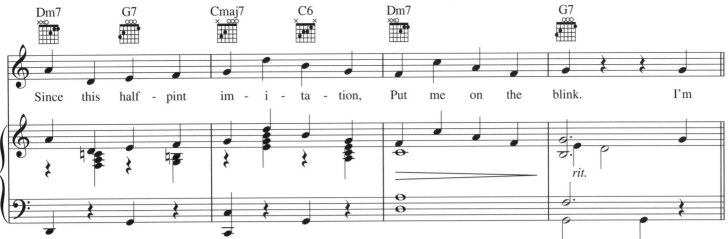

Since this half-pint im-i-ta-tion, Put me on the blink. I'm

rit.

Slowly

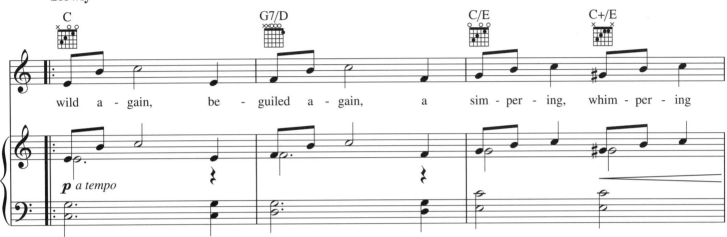

wild a-gain, be-guiled a-gain, a sim-per-ing, whim-per-ing

p a tempo

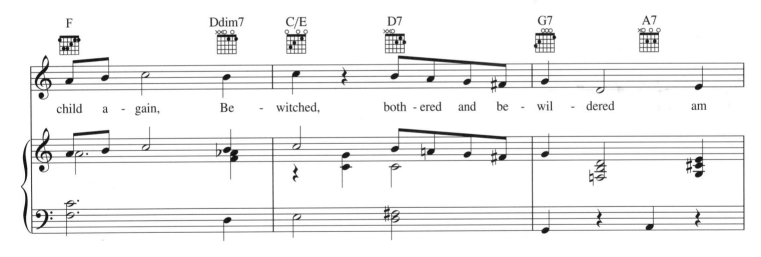

child a-gain, Be-witched, both-ered and be-wil-dered am

mf

I.

Could-n't sleep, and would-n't sleep, When

mf

p

love came and told me I should - n't sleep, Be - witched, both - ered and be -

wil - dered am I. _____

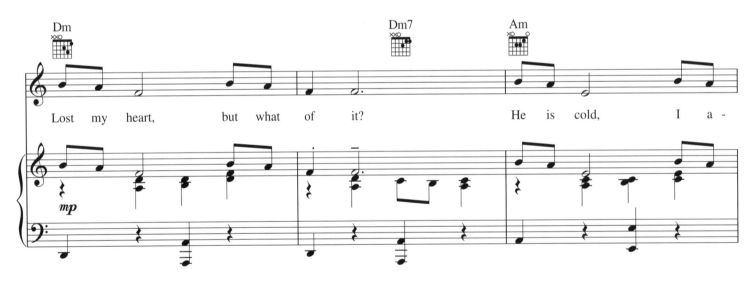

Lost my heart, but what of it? He is cold, I a -

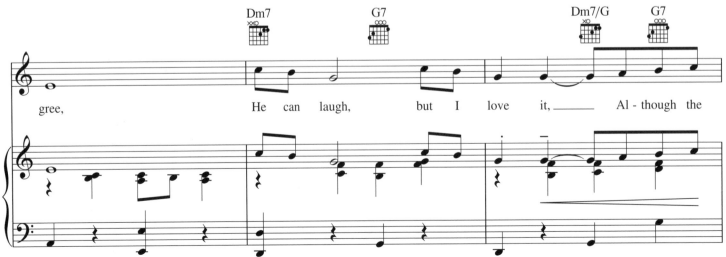

gree, He can laugh, but I love it, _____ Al - though the

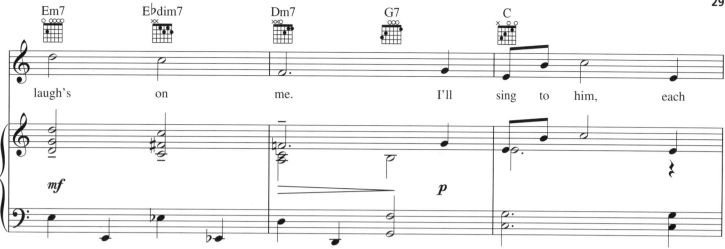

laugh's on me. I'll sing to him, each

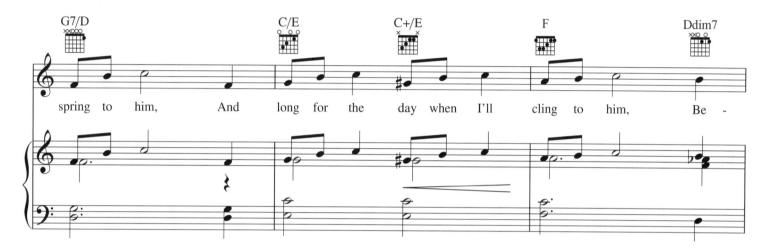

spring to him, And long for the day when I'll cling to him, Be -

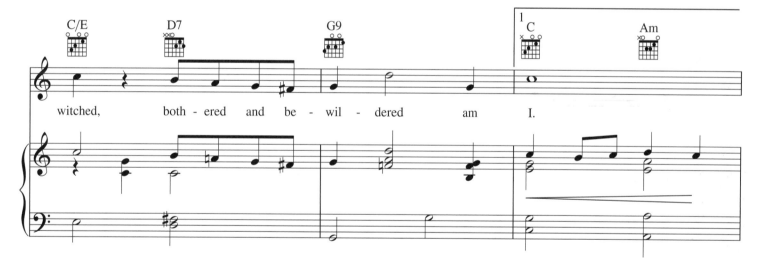

witched, both - ered and be - wil - dered am I.

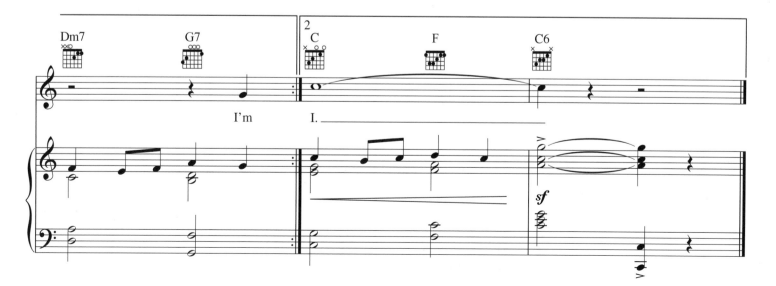

I'm I.

THE BIRTH OF THE BLUES

from GEORGE WHITE'S SCANDALS OF 1926

Words by B.G. DeSYLVA and LEW BROWN
Music by RAY HENDERSON

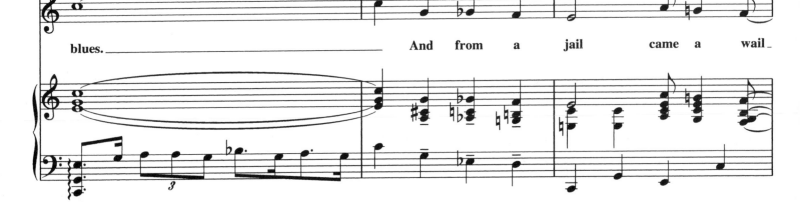

BLUES IN THE NIGHT
(My Mama Done Tol' Me)
from BLUES IN THE NIGHT

Words by JOHNNY MERCER
Music by HAROLD ARLEN

Nat - chez to Mo - bile, from Mem - phis to St. Joe, wher -

ev - er the four winds blow; I

been in some big towns an' heard me some big talk,

but there is one thing I know, a a

CALL ME

Words and Music by
TONY HATCH

If you're feel-ing sad and lone-ly, there's a serv-ice I

can ren-der. Tell the one who loves you on-ly,

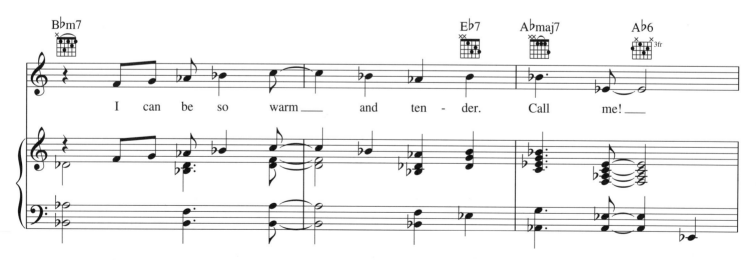

I can be so warm and ten-der. Call me!

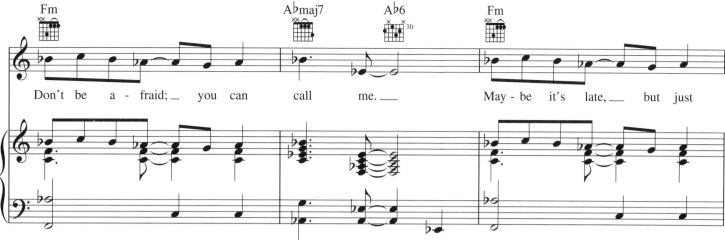

May - be that's be - cause __ I love you. Call me! __

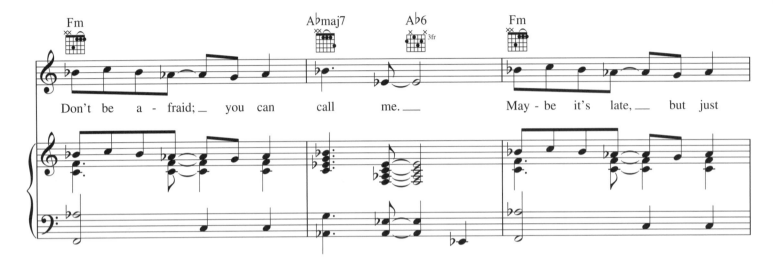

Don't be a - fraid; __ you can call me. __ May - be it's late, __ but just

call me. __ Tell me and I'll __ be a - round. __

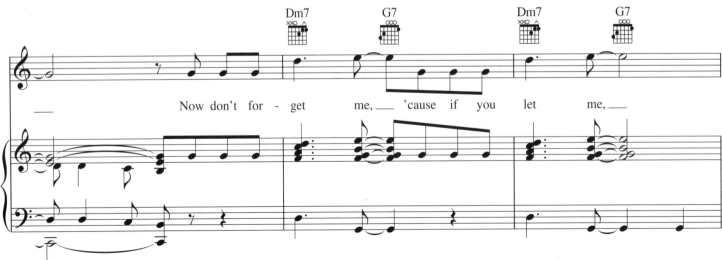

Now don't for - get me, __ 'cause if you let me, __

I will al-ways stay by you. You got-ta trust me;____ that's how it

must be.____ There's so much that I can do._____

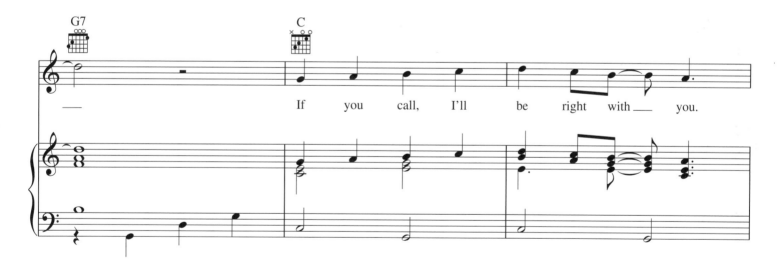

If you call, I'll be right with____ you.

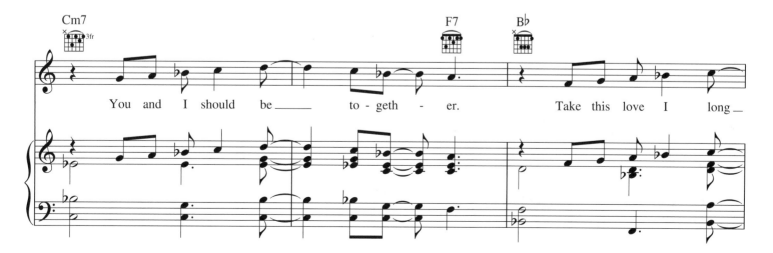

You and I should be_____ to-geth - er. Take this love I long____

to give you, I'll be at your side for - ev - er.

Call me! Don't be a - fraid; you can call me.

May - be it's late, but just call me. Tell me and I'll be a -

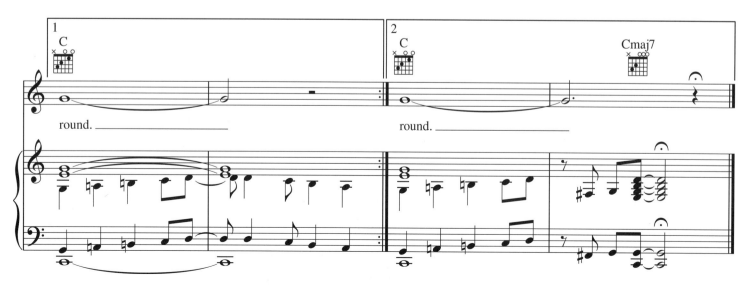

round. round.

CAN'T HELP LOVIN' DAT MAN

from SHOW BOAT

Lyrics by OSCAR HAMMERSTEIN II
Music by JEROME KERN

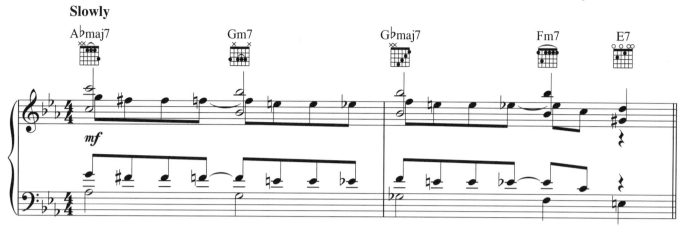

Fish got to swim and birds got to fly, I got to love one
Tell me he's la-zy, tell me he's slow, tell me I'm cra-zy,

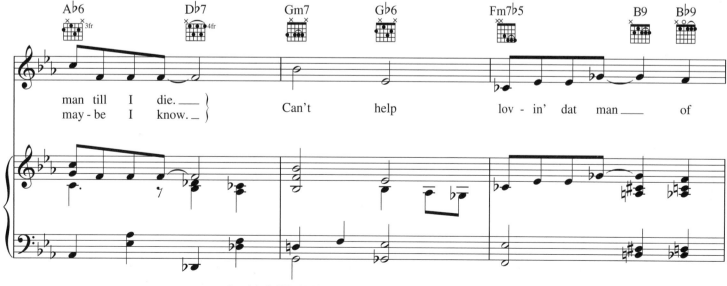

man till I die.
may-be I know. Can't help lov-in' dat man of

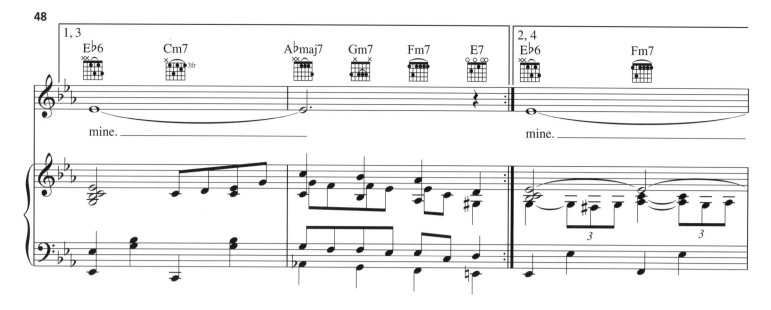

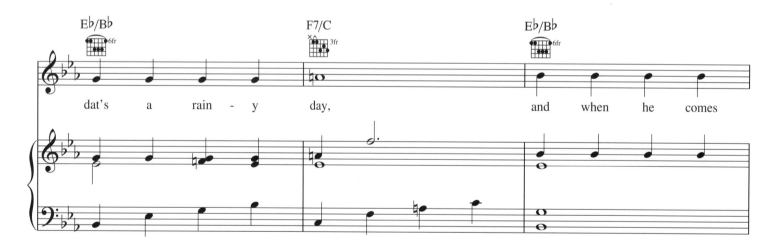

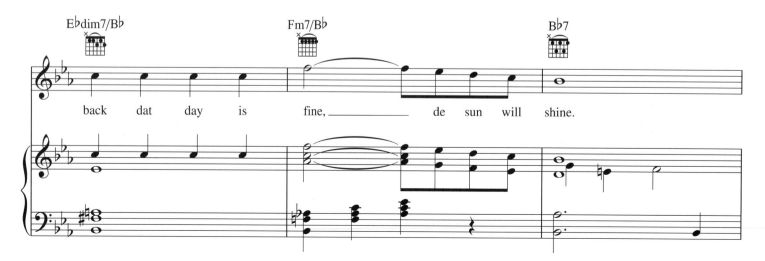

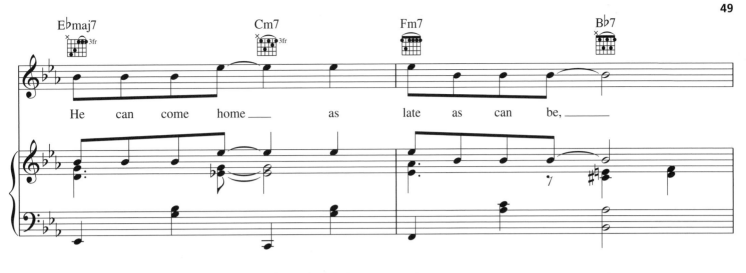

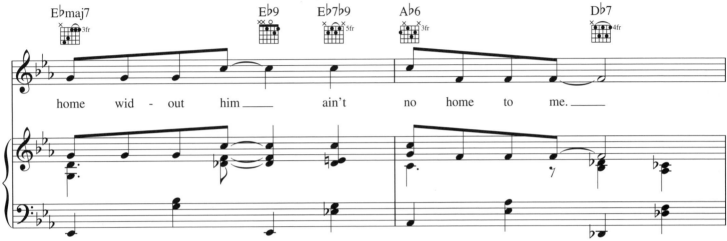

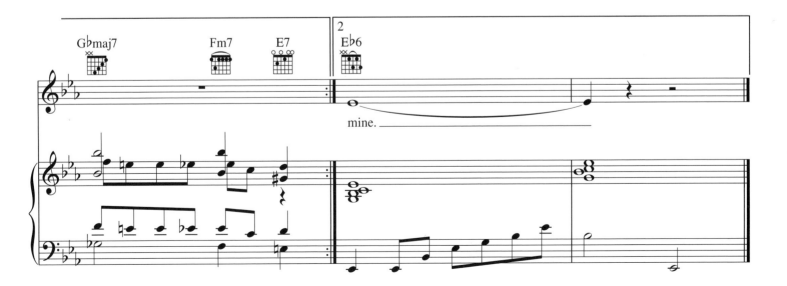

CHEROKEE
(Indian Love Song)

Words and Music by
RAY NOBLE

Moderately bright Swing

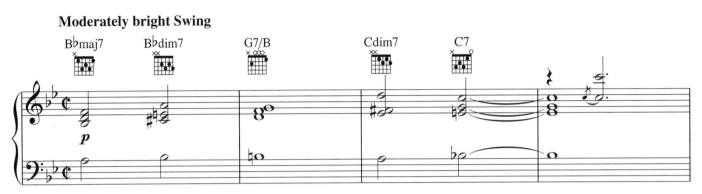

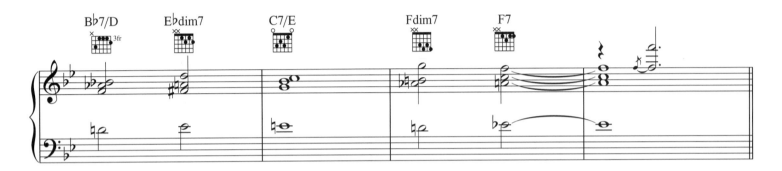

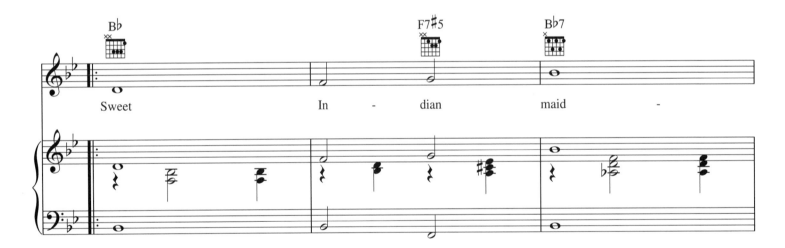

Sweet In - dian maid - en, since first I met

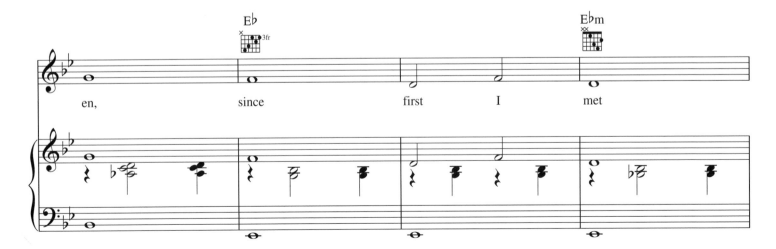

en, since first I met

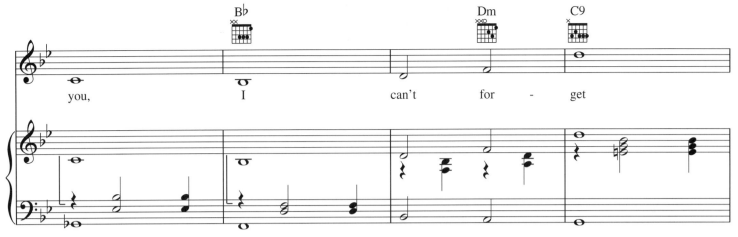

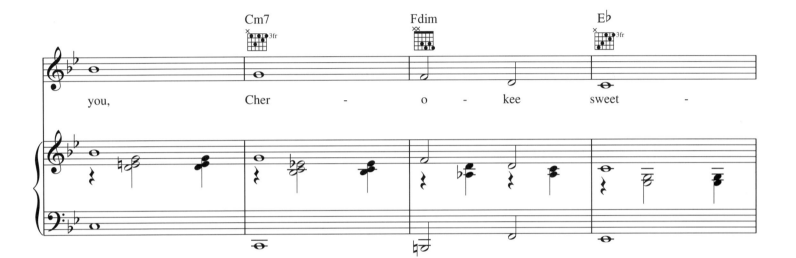

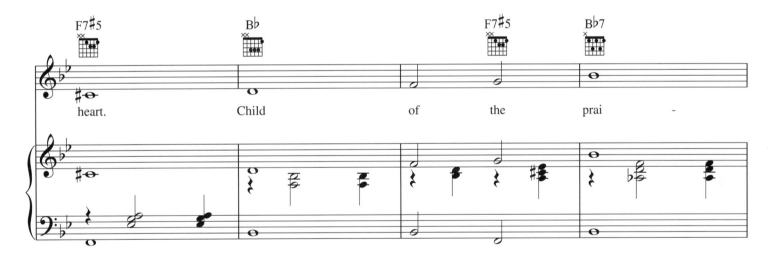

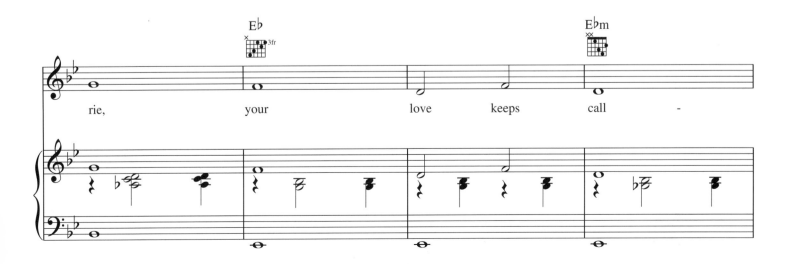

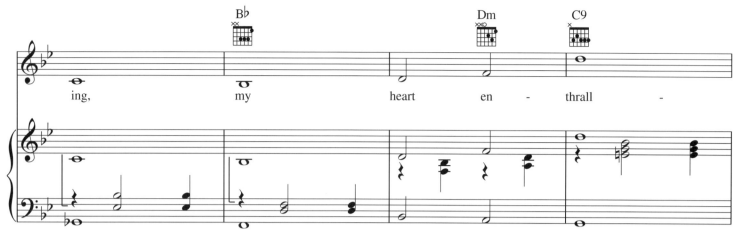

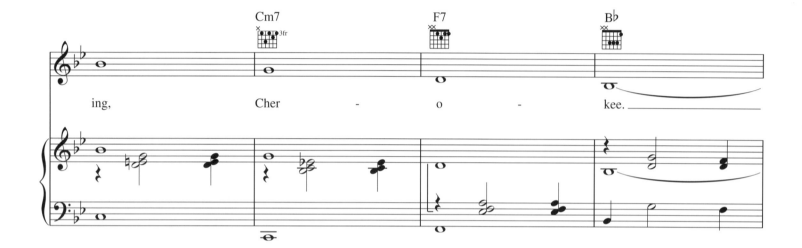

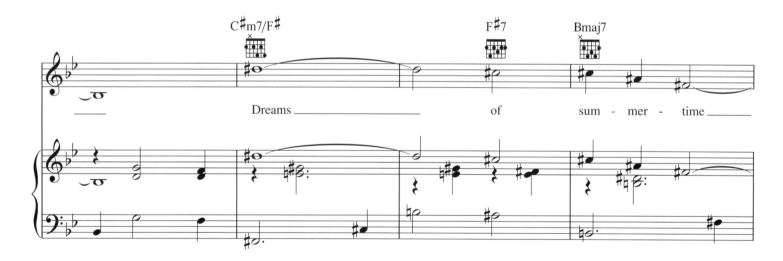

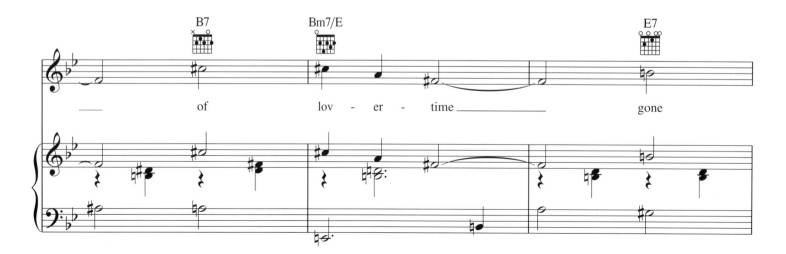

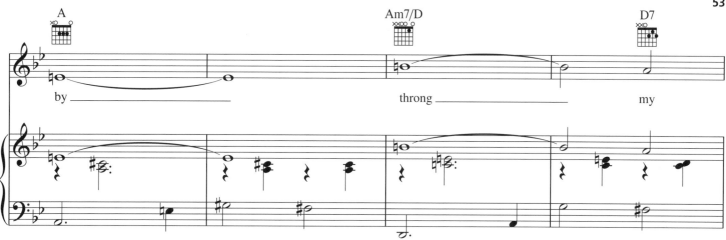

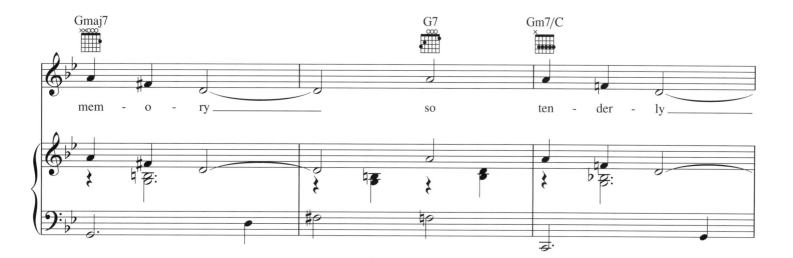

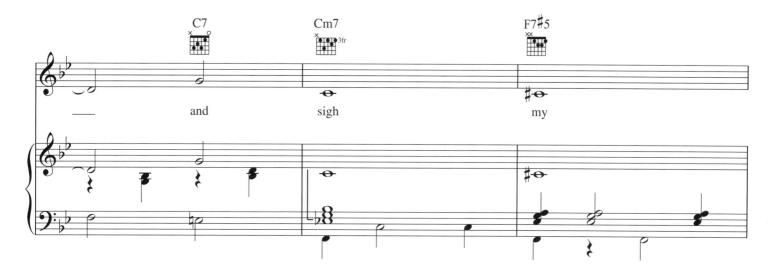

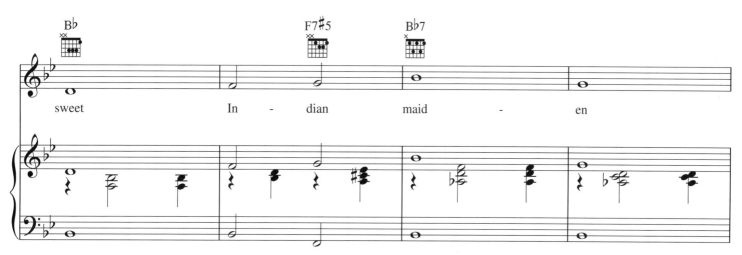

one day I'll hold you,

in my arms fold you,

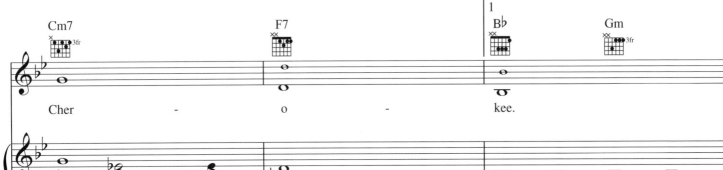

Cher - o - kee.

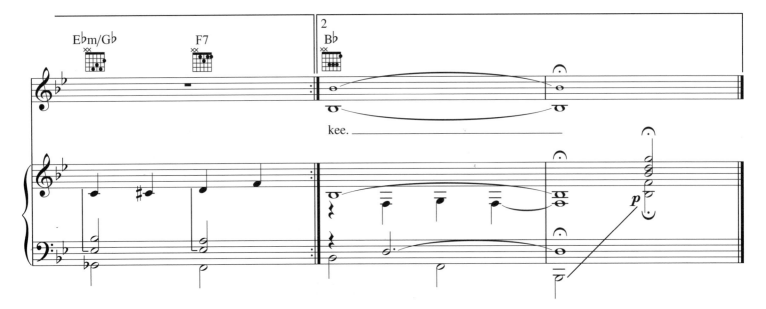

kee.

DARN THAT DREAM

Lyric by EDDIE DE LANGE
Music by JIMMY VAN HEUSEN

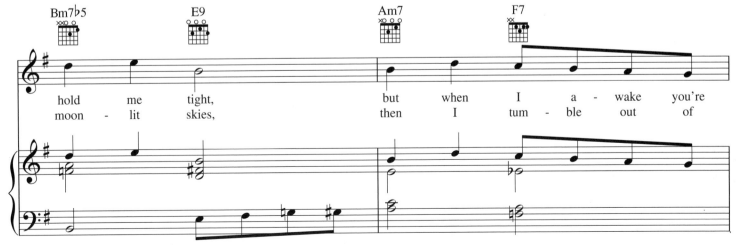

Darn that dream I
Darn your lips and

dream each night, you say you love me and you
darn your eyes, they lift me high a- bove the

hold me tight, but when I a- wake you're
moon - lit skies, then I tum - ble out of

wel-come a nice ___ old night - mare. Darn that dream and

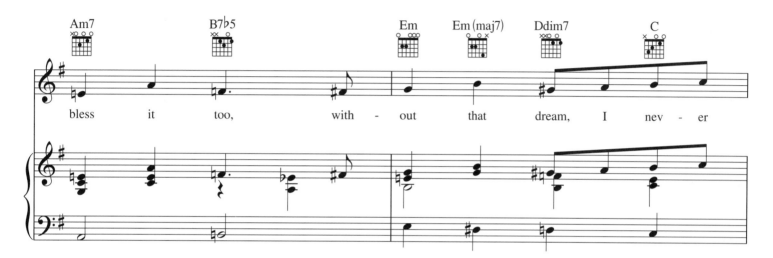

bless it too, with - out that dream, I nev - er

would have you. But it haunts me and it

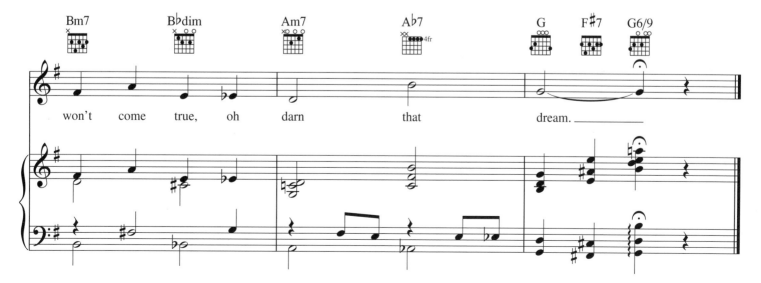

won't come true, oh darn that dream. ___

DAYS OF WINE AND ROSES

Lyric by JOHNNY MERCER
Music by HENRY MANCINI

DEARLY BELOVED

from YOU WERE NEVER LOVELIER

Music by JEROME KERN
Words by JOHNNY MERCER

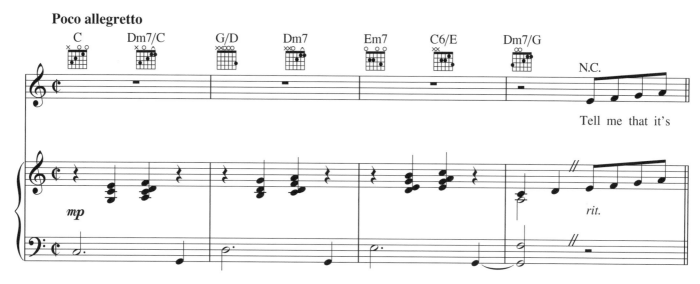

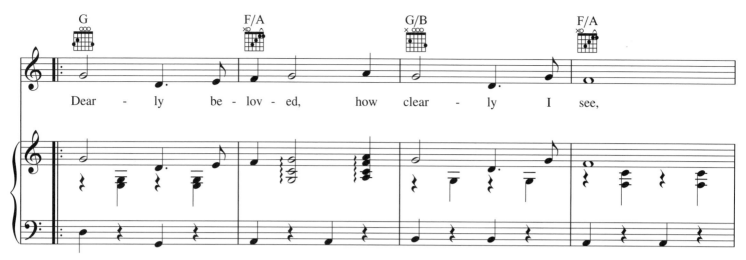

Dear - ly be - lov - ed, how clear - ly I see,

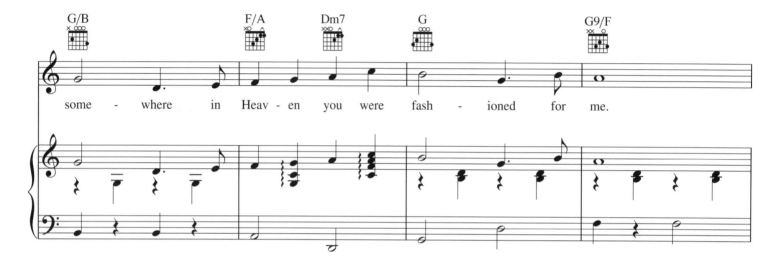

some - where in Heav - en you were fash - ioned for me.

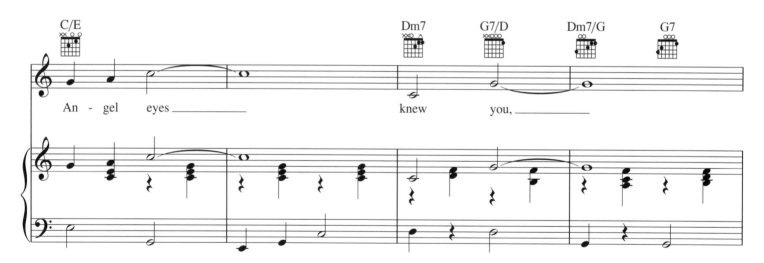

An - gel eyes _____ knew you, _____

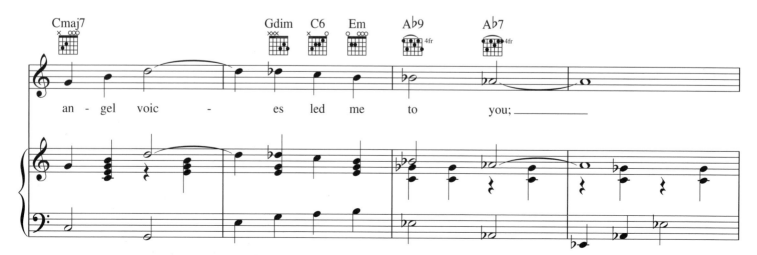

an - gel voic - es led me to you; _____

EASY TO LOVE
(You'd Be So Easy to Love)
from BORN TO DANCE

Words and Music by
COLE PORTER

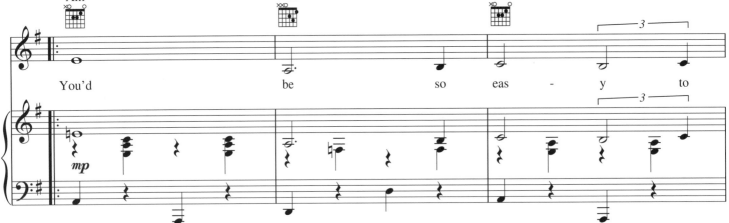

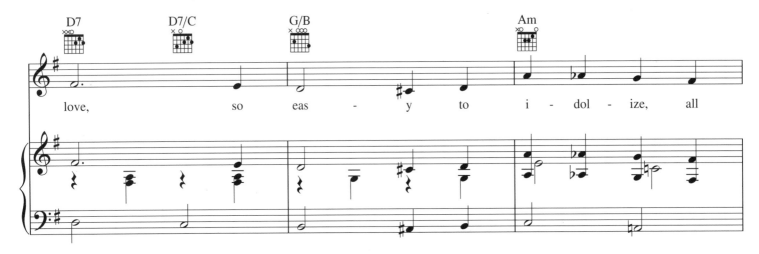

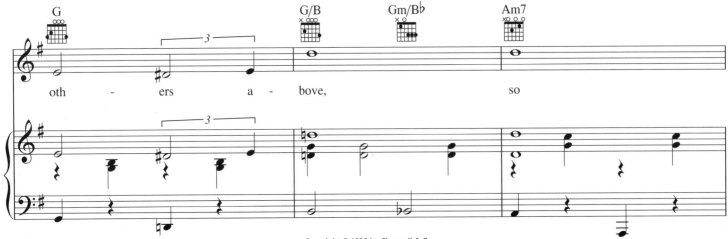

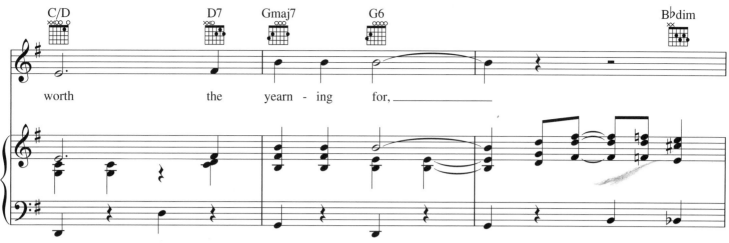

worth the yearn-ing for, _____

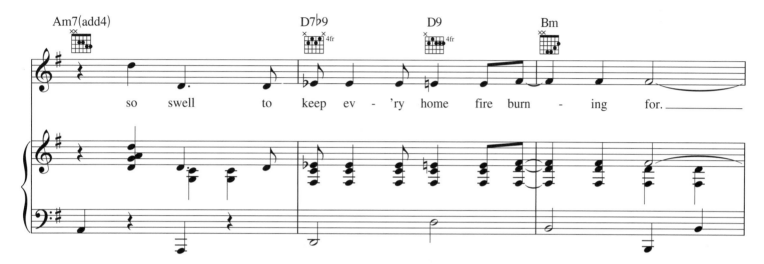

so swell to keep ev-'ry home fire burn - ing for. _____

We'd be so

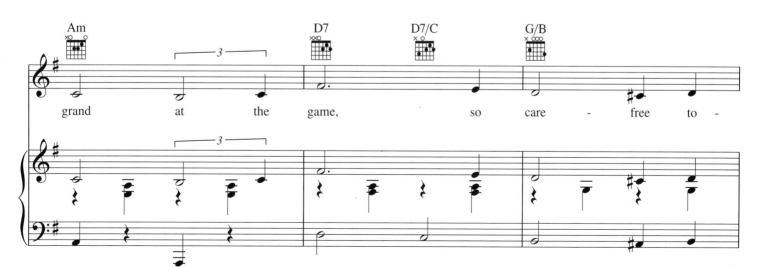

grand at the game, so care - free to -

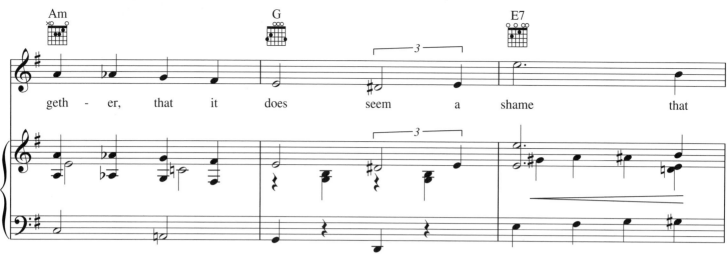

geth - er, that it does seem a shame that

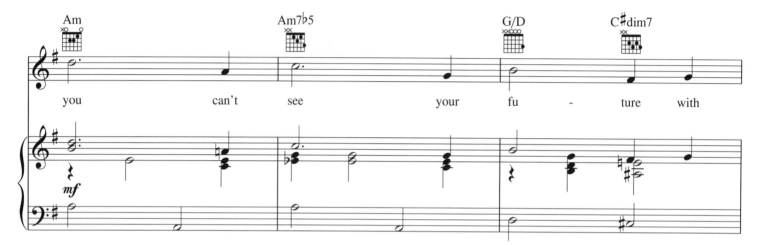

you can't see your fu - ture with

me, 'cause you'd be oh, so eas - y to

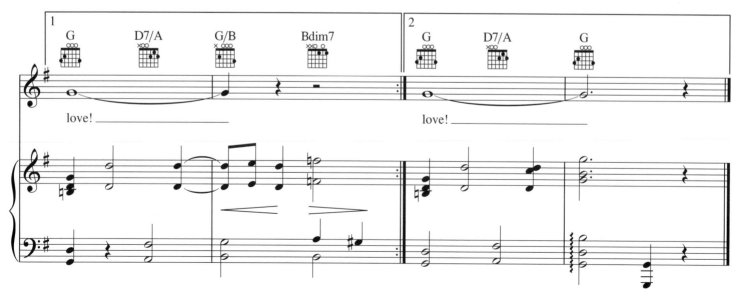

love! _____ love! _____

THE END OF A LOVE AFFAIR

Words and Music by
EDWARD C. REDDING

heart, and not my mind, is boss!

D.S. al Coda

a tempo

So I

CODA

fair?

a tempo

FALLING IN LOVE WITH LOVE
from THE BOYS FROM SYRACUSE

Words by LORENZ HART
Music by RICHARD RODGERS

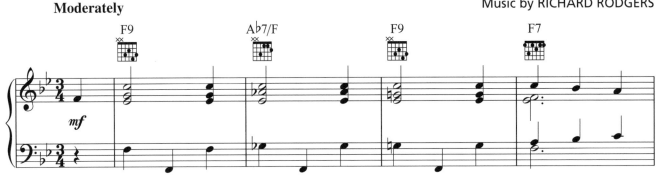

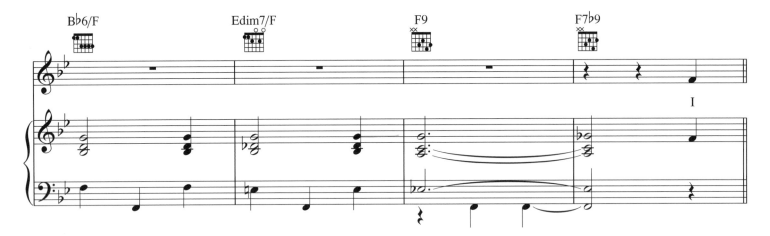

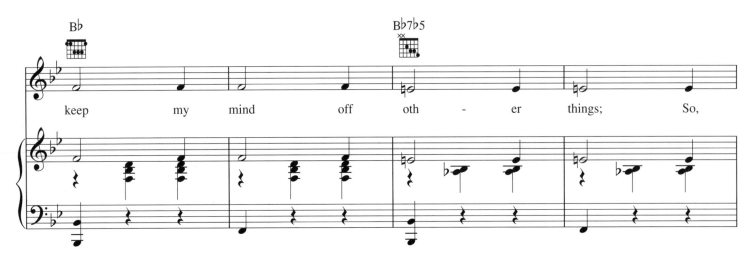

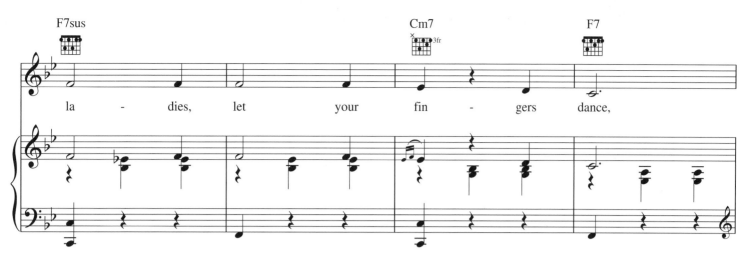

la - dies, let your fin - gers dance,

And

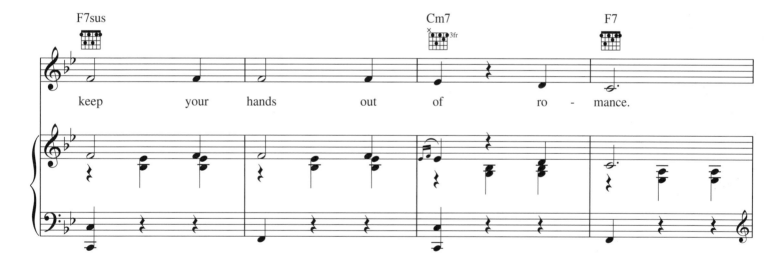

keep your hands out of ro - mance.

Love - ly

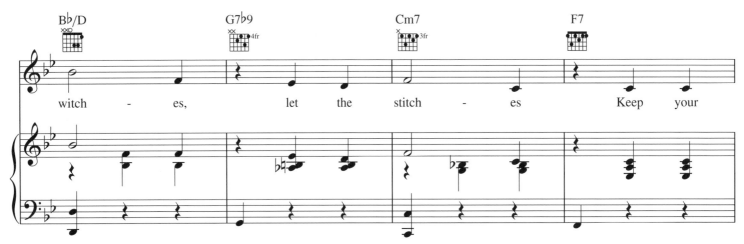

witch - es, let the stitch - es Keep your

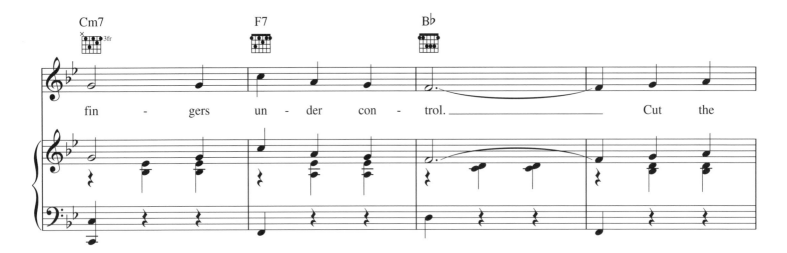

fin - gers un - der con - trol. _____ Cut the

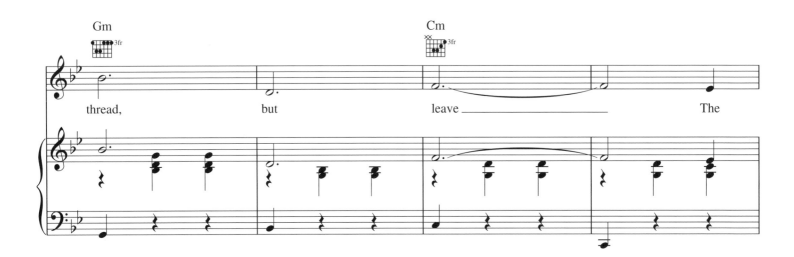

thread, but leave _____ The

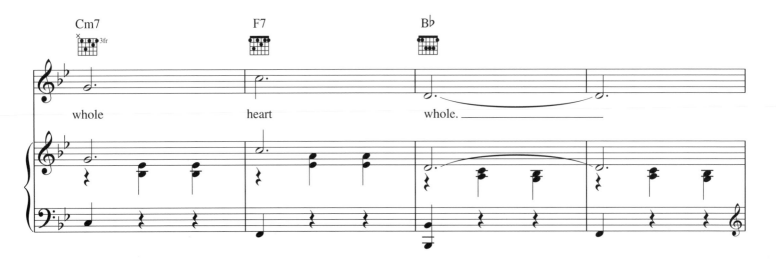

whole heart whole. _____ The

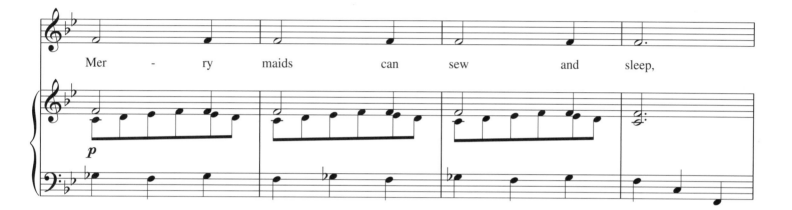

Mer - ry maids can sew and sleep,

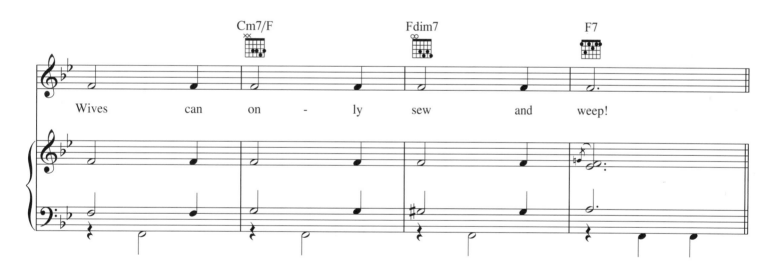

Wives can on - ly sew and weep!

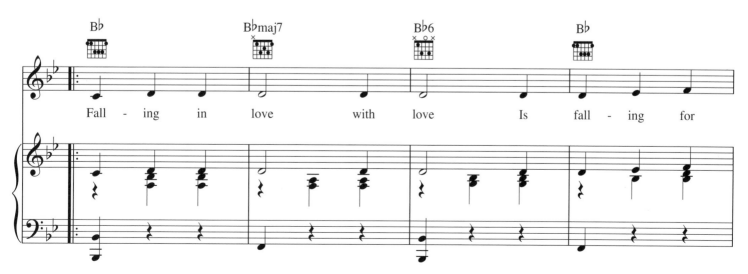

Fall - ing in love with love Is fall - ing for

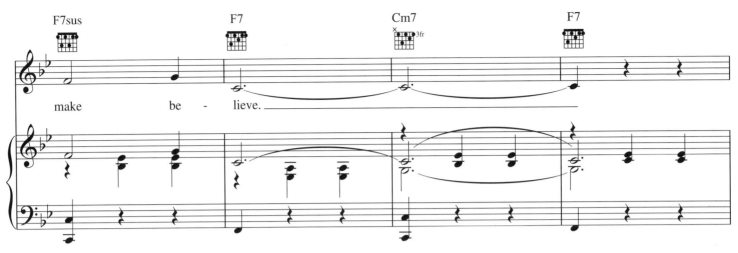

make be - lieve. ____

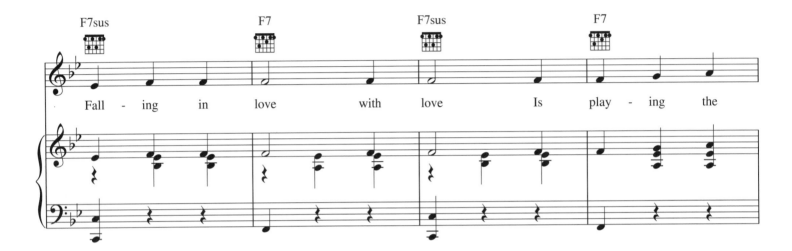

Fall - ing in love with love Is play - ing the

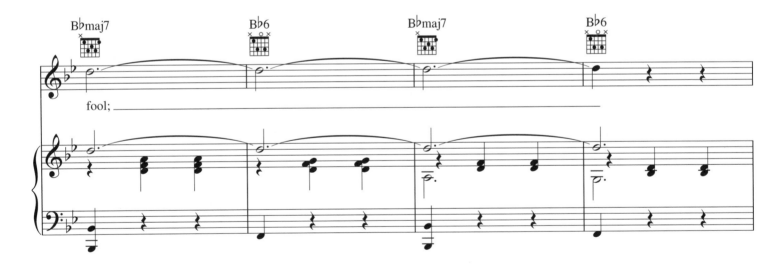

fool; ____

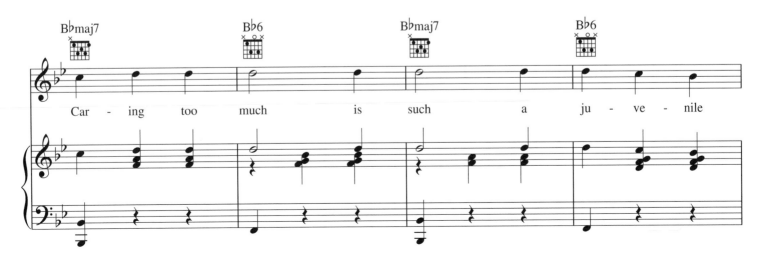

Car - ing too much is such a ju - ve - nile

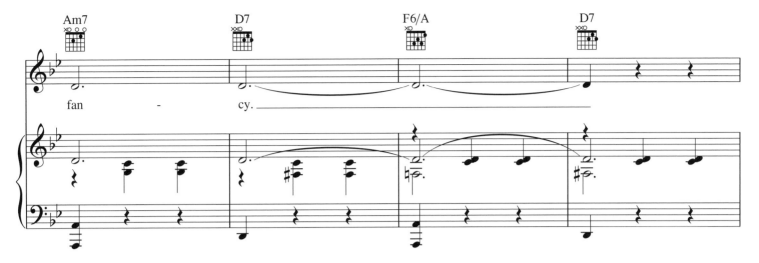

fan - cy. _____

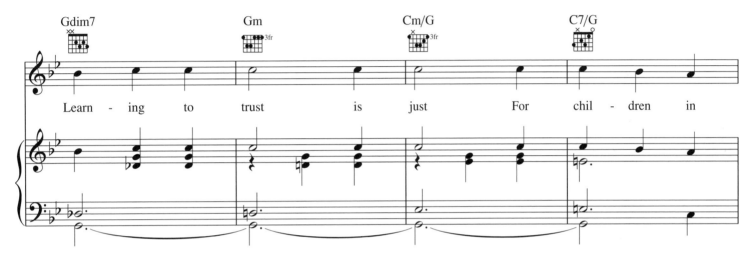

Learn - ing to trust is just For chil - dren in

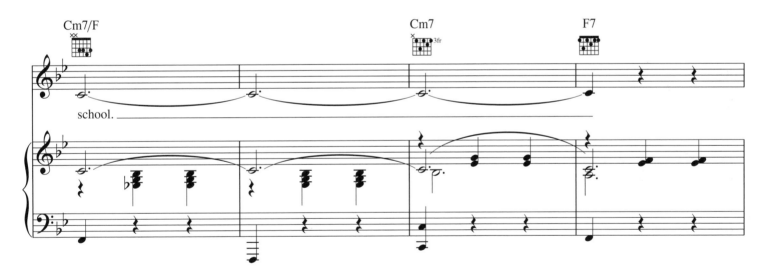

school. _____

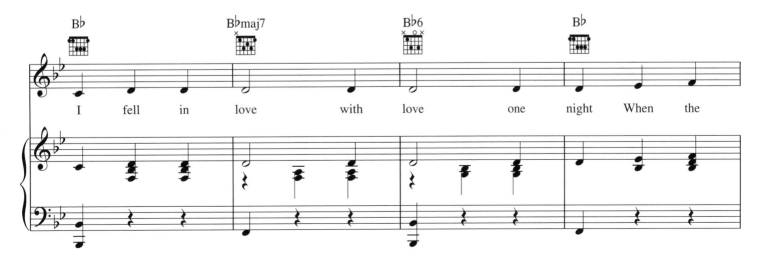

I fell in love with love one night When the

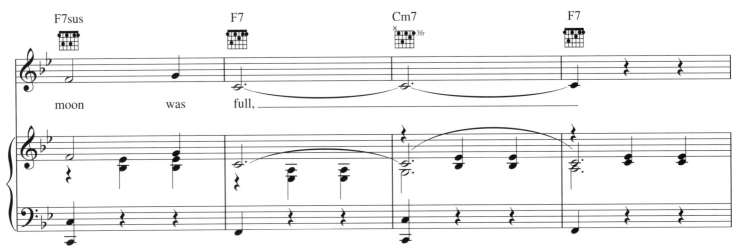

moon was full, _____

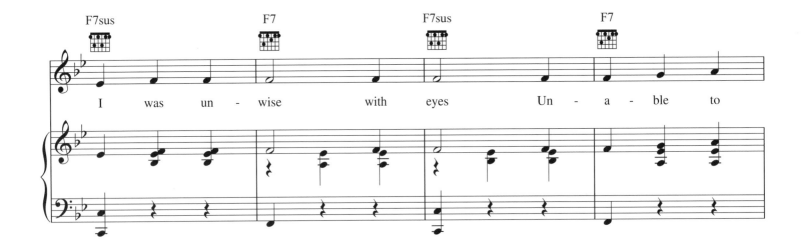

I was un - wise with eyes Un - a - ble to

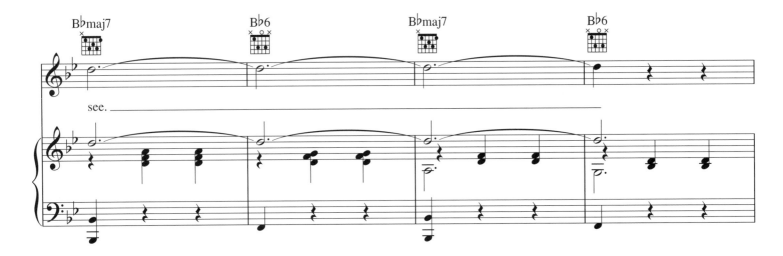

see. _____

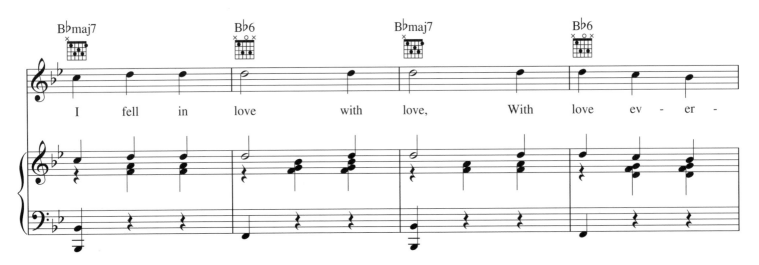

I fell in love with love, With love ev - er -

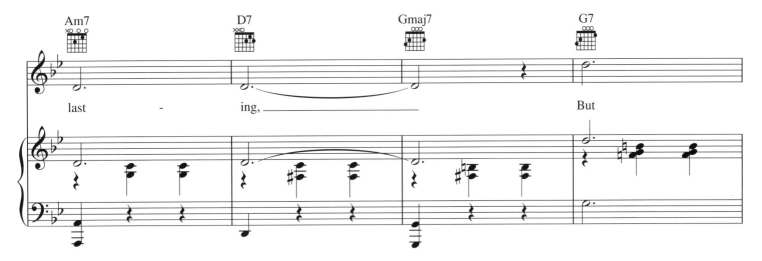

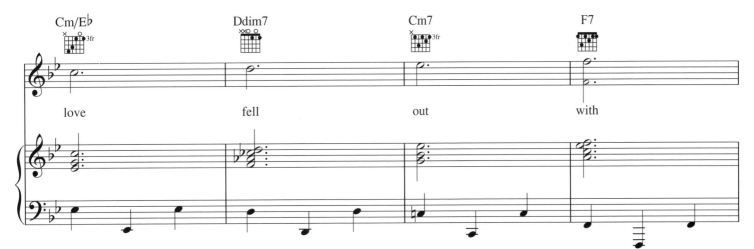

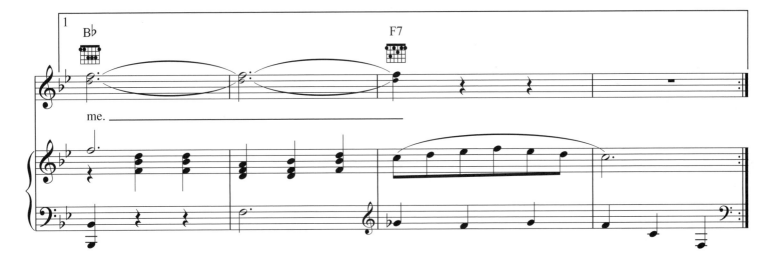

A FINE ROMANCE

from SWING TIME

Words by DOROTHY FIELDS
Music by JEROME KERN

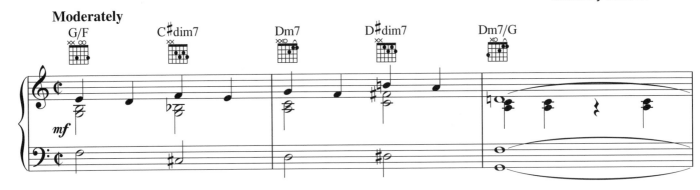

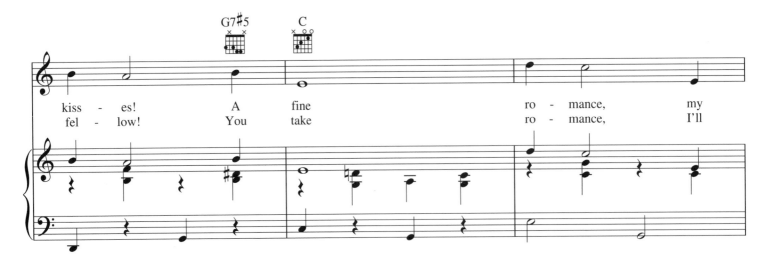

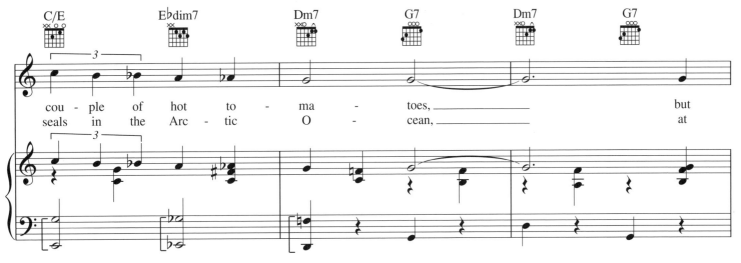

couple of hot to-ma-toes, _____ but
seals in the Arc-tic O-cean, _____ at

you're as cold as yes-ter-day's mashed po-ta-toes. _____
least they cold flap their fins to ex-press e-mo-tion. _____

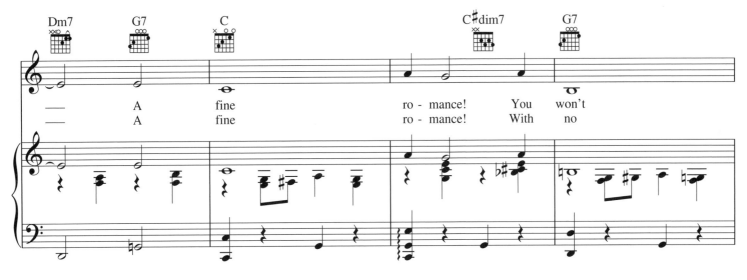

_____ A fine ro-mance! You won't
_____ A fine ro-mance! With no

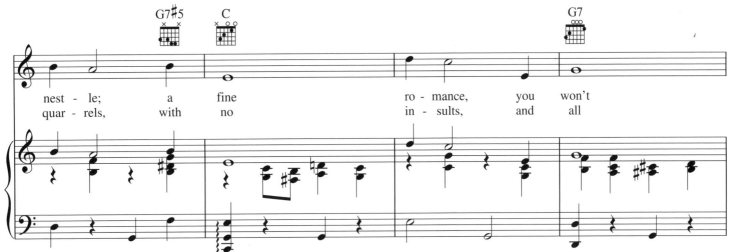

nest-le; a fine ro-mance, you won't
quar-rels, with no in-sults, and all

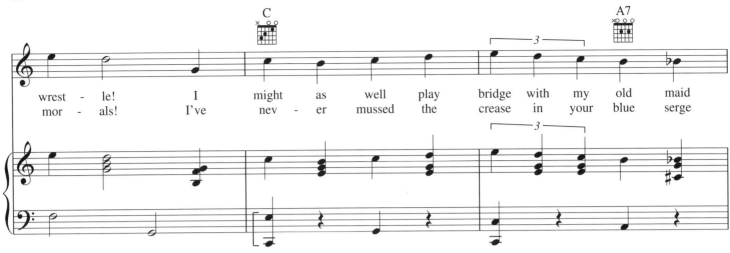

wrest - le!   I   might as well play   bridge with my old maid
mor - als!   I've   nev - er mussed the   crease in your blue serge

aunts!   I have - n't got   a   chance.
pants,   I   nev - er get the   chance.

This   is   a   fine ro - mance!
This   is   a   fine ro -

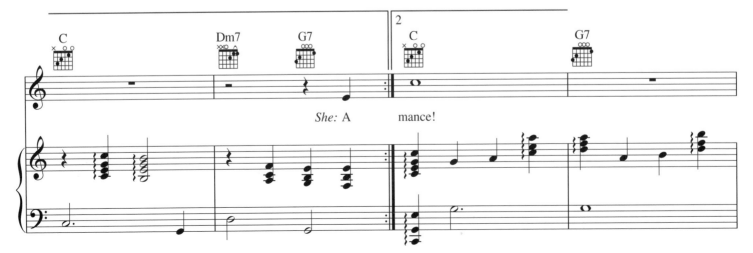

She: A   mance!

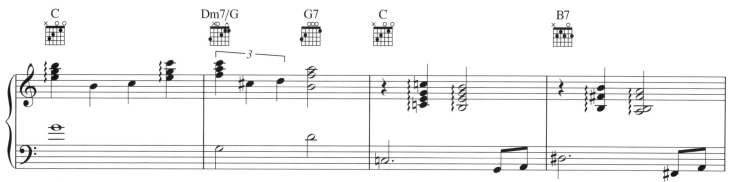

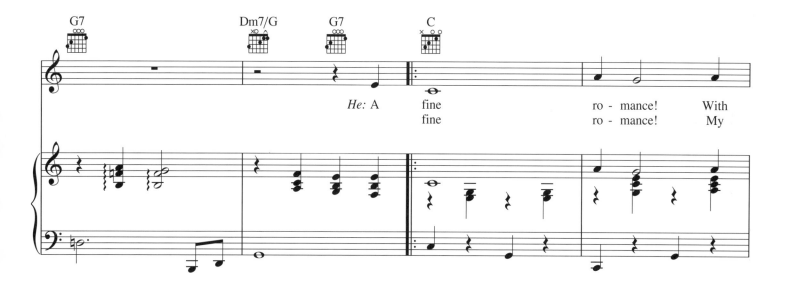

He: A fine ro - mance! With
fine ro - mance! My

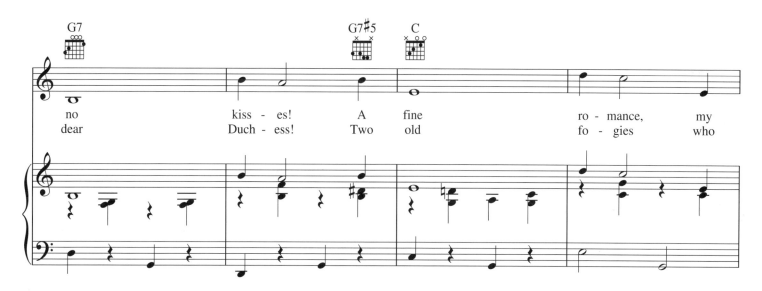

no kiss - es! A fine ro - mance, my
dear Duch - ess! A Two old fo - gies who

friend, this is! We two should be like
need crutch - es! True love should have like the

THE FOLKS WHO LIVE ON THE HILL

from HIGH, WIDE AND HANDSOME

Lyrics by OSCAR HAMMERSTEIN II
Music by JEROME KERN

GOD BLESS' THE CHILD

from BUBBLING BROWN SUGAR

Words and Music by ARTHUR HERZOG JR.
and BILLIE HOLIDAY

THE GIRL FROM IPANEMA
(Garôta de Ipanema)

Music by ANTONIO CARLOS JOBIM
English Words by NORMAN GIMBEL
Original Words by VINICIUS DE MORAES

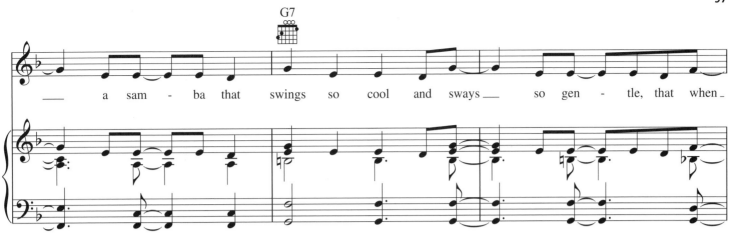

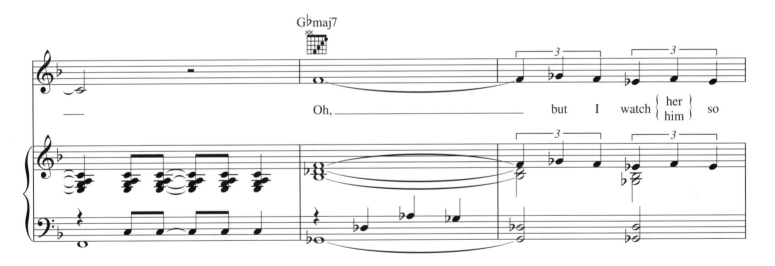

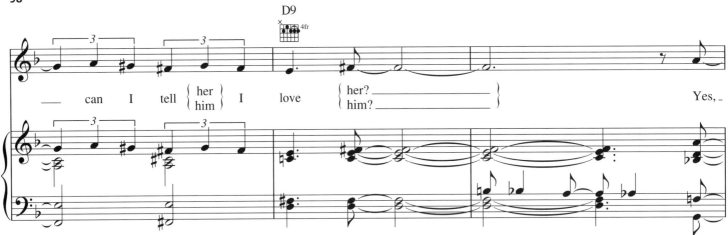

can I tell {her / him} I love {her? / him?} Yes,

I would give my heart glad - ly,

but each day when {she / he} walks to the sea, {she / he}

looks straight a - head not at me. Tall and tan and young

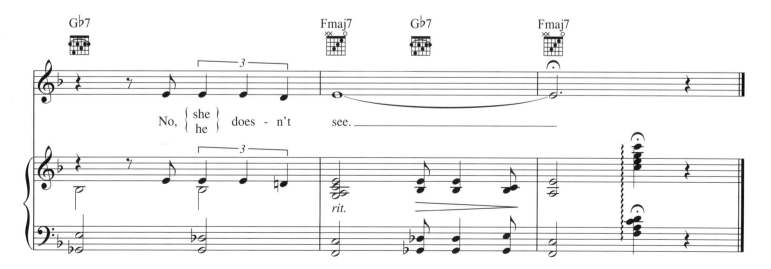

HARLEM NOCTURNE

Music by EARLE HAGEN
Words by DICK ROGERS

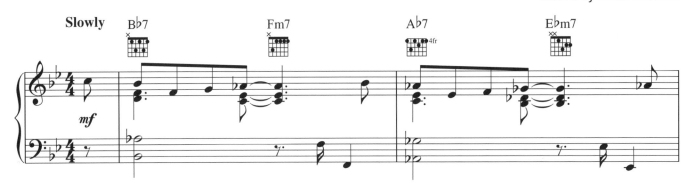

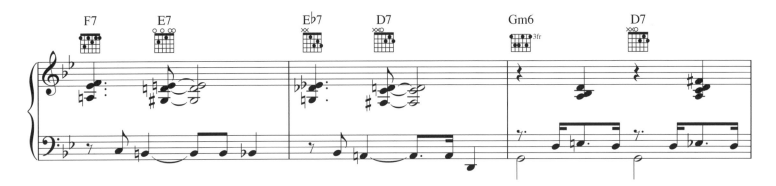

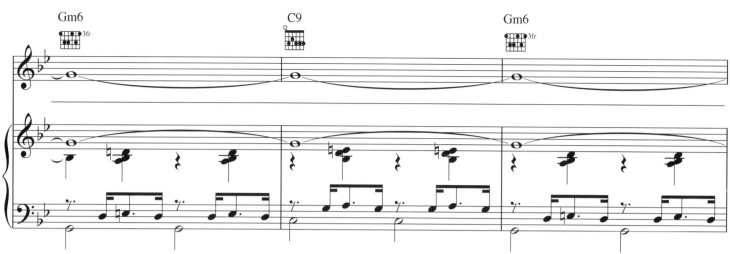

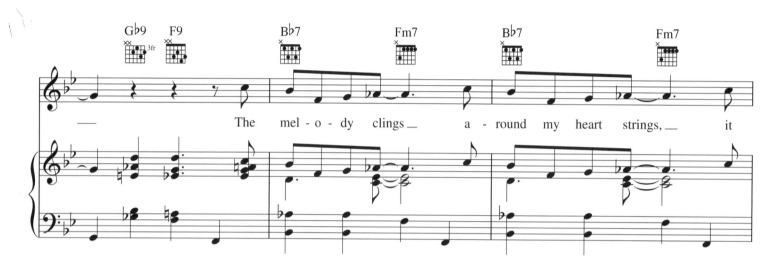

The mel-o-dy clings __ a-round my heart strings, __ it

won't let me go __ when I'm lone-ly. __ I

hear it in dreams __ and some-how it seems __ it

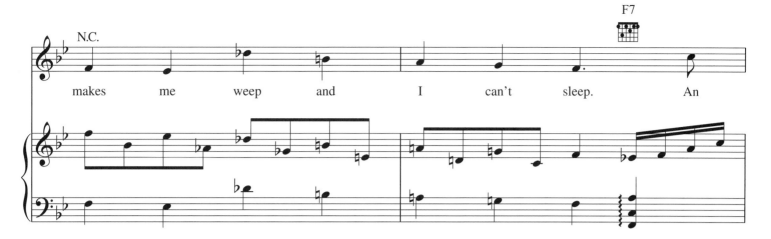

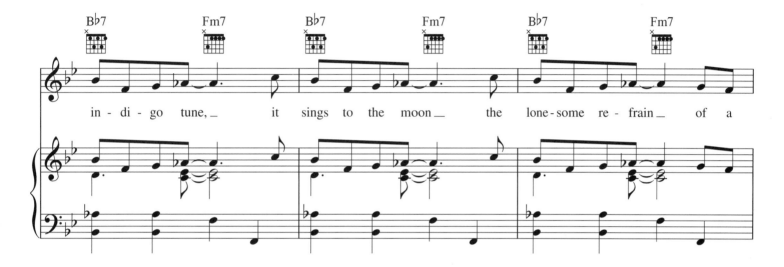

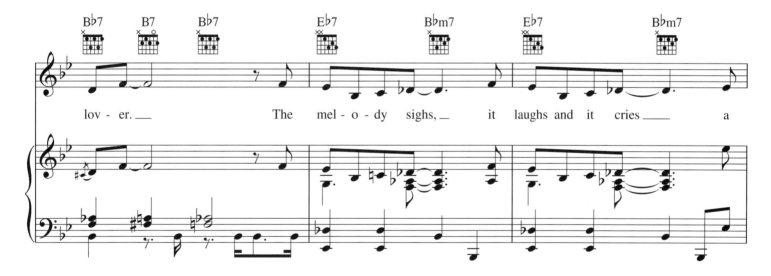

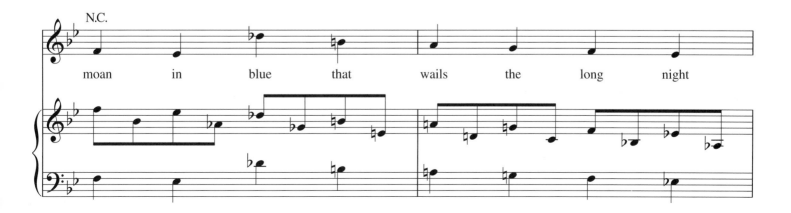

HONEYSUCKLE ROSE

from AIN'T MISBEHAVIN'
from TIN PAN ALLEY

Words by ANDY RAZAF
Music by THOMAS "FATS" WALLER

Moderately, with a lift

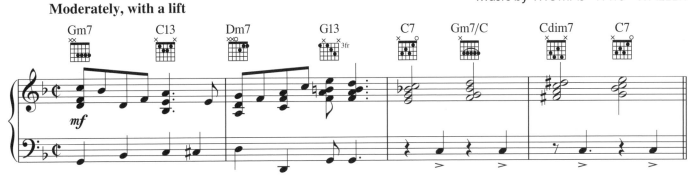

Ev-'ry hon-ey-bee fills with jeal-ou-sy when they see you out with

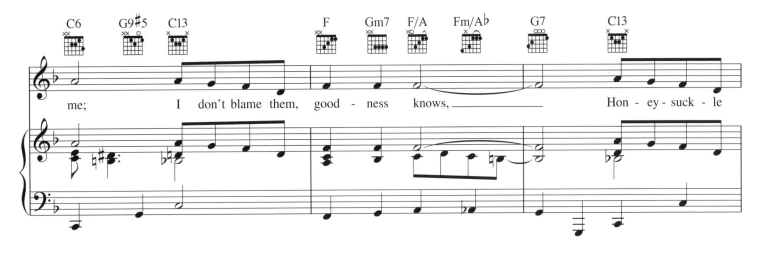

me; I don't blame them, good-ness knows, _____ Hon-ey-suck-le

Rose. When you're pass-in' by

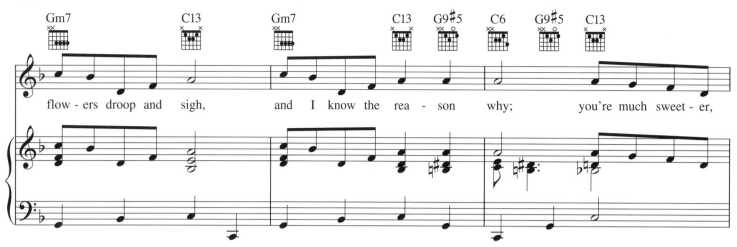

flow - ers droop and sigh, and I know the rea - son why; you're much sweet - er,

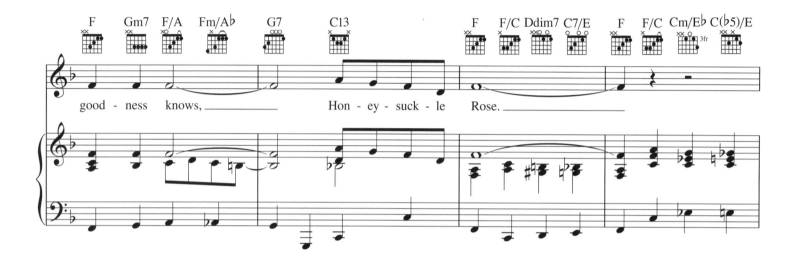

good - ness knows, Hon - ey - suck - le Rose.

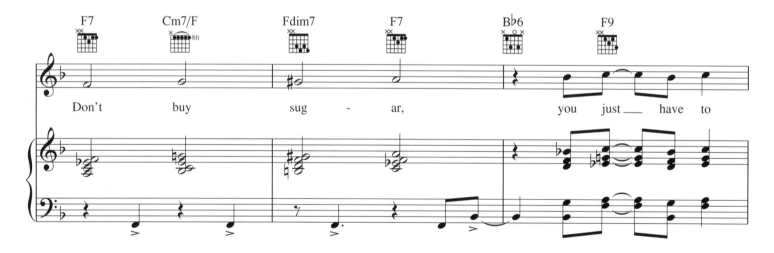

Don't buy sug - ar, you just — have to

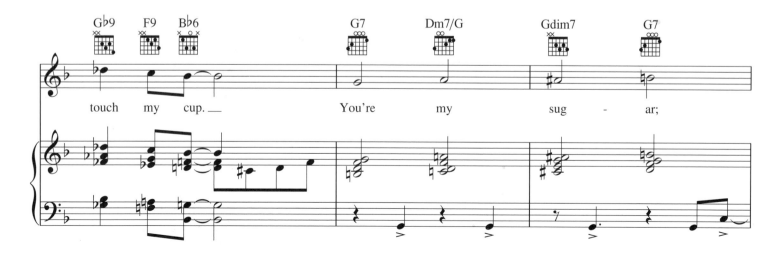

touch my cup. You're my sug - ar;

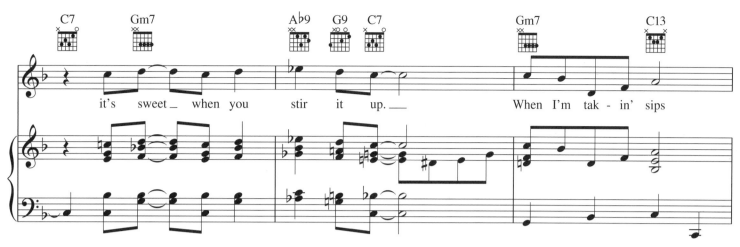

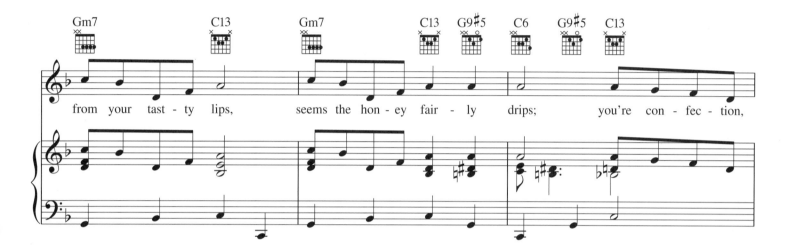

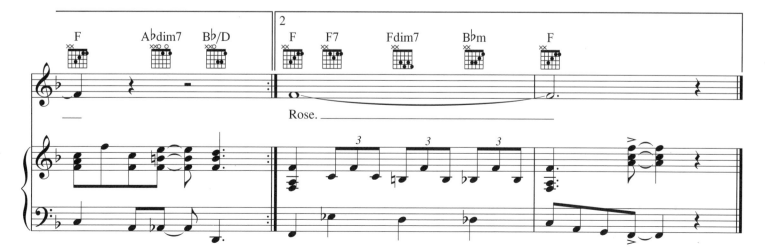

HAVE YOU MET MISS JONES?

from I'D RATHER BE RIGHT

Words by LORENZ HART
Music by RICHARD RODGERS

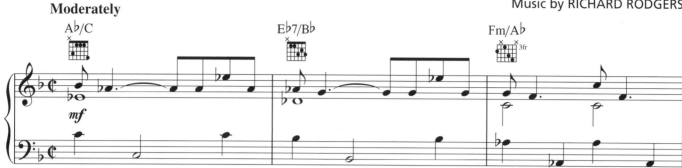

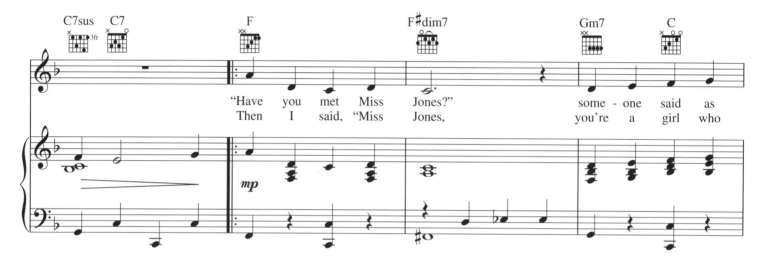

"Have you met Miss Jones?" some-one said as
Then I said, "Miss Jones, you're a girl who

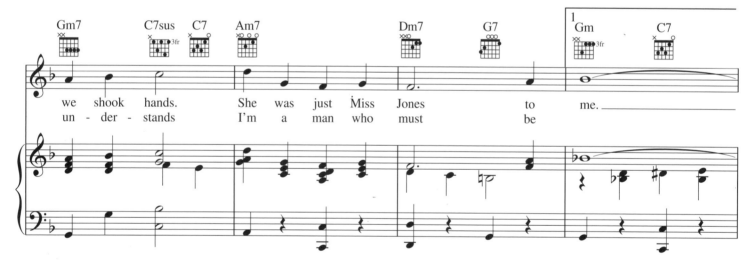

we shook hands. She was just Miss Jones to me. ___
un-der-stands I'm a man who must to be

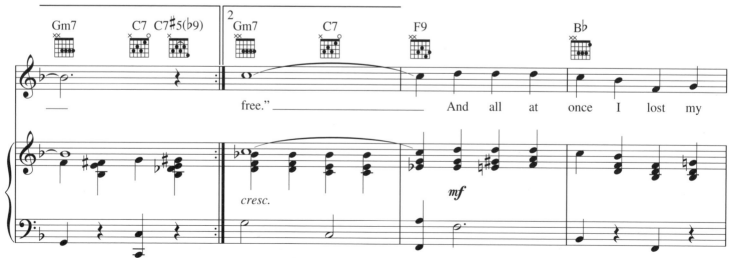

free." ___ And all at once I lost my

breath, and all at once was scared to death, and all at once I owned the

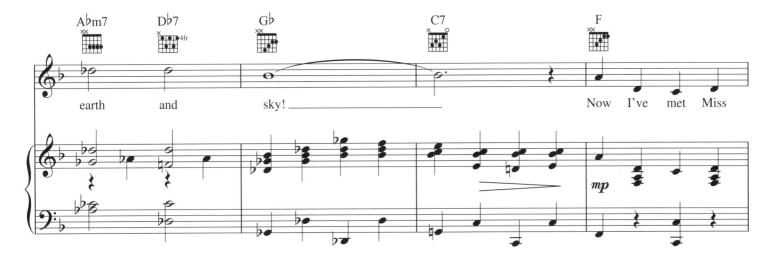

earth and sky! _____ Now I've met Miss

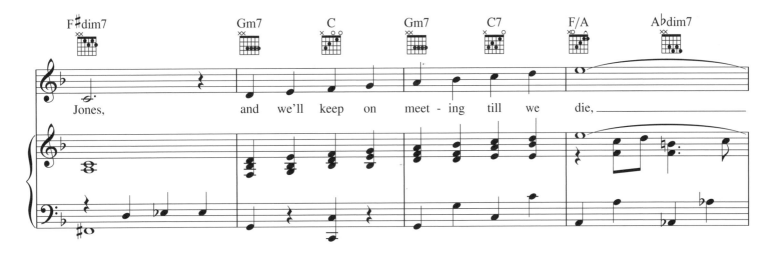

Jones, and we'll keep on meet- ing till we die, _____

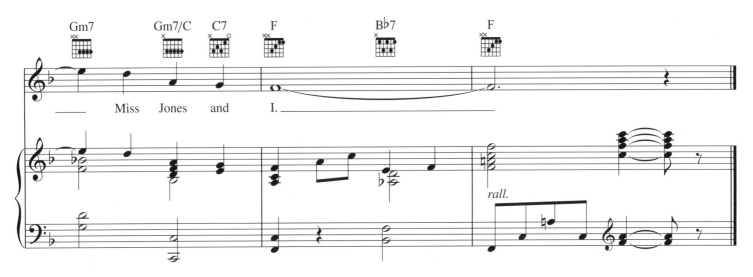

____ Miss Jones and I. _____

HELLO, YOUNG LOVERS
from THE KING AND I

Lyrics by OSCAR HAMMERSTEIN II
Music by RICHARD RODGERS

Molto moderato

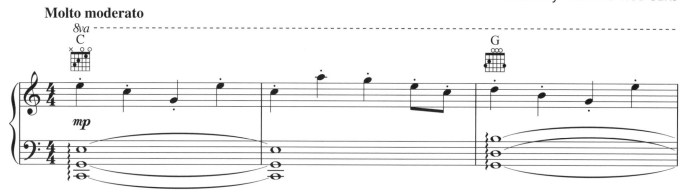

Slowly

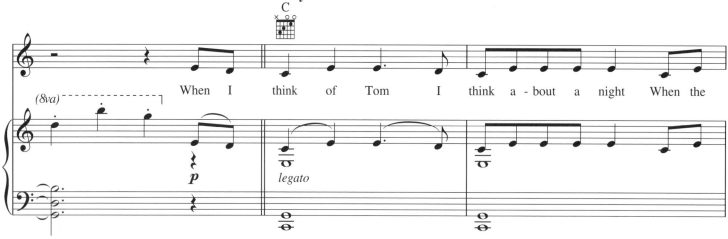

When I think of Tom I think a-bout a night When the

earth smelled of sum-mer, And the sky was streaked with white, And the soft mist of Eng-land was

sleep-ing on a hill; I re-mem-ber this ____ And I al-ways

will. _____ There are new lov - ers now on the

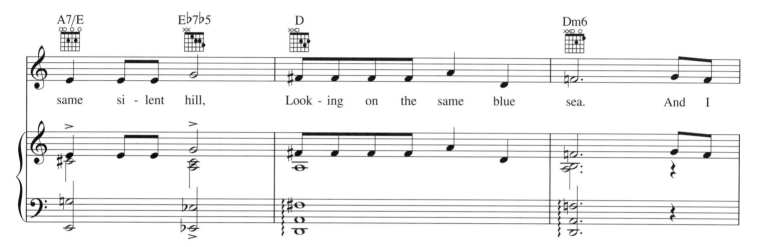

same si - lent hill, Look - ing on the same blue sea. And I

know Tom and I are a part of them all, And they're all a part of Tom _____

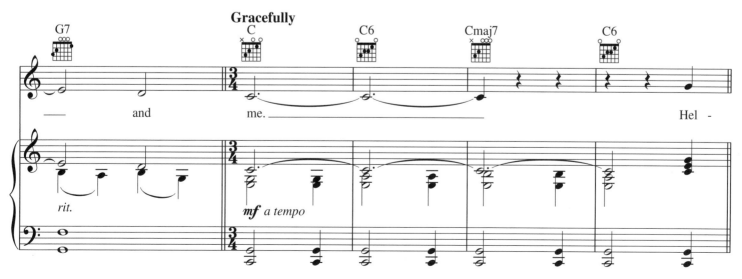

Gracefully

___ and me. _____ Hel -

Refrain *(very moderately)*

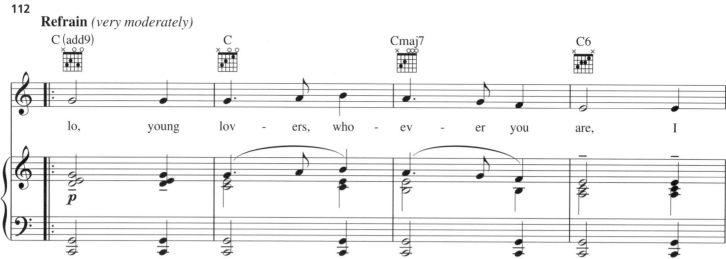

lo, young lov-ers, who-ev-er you are, I

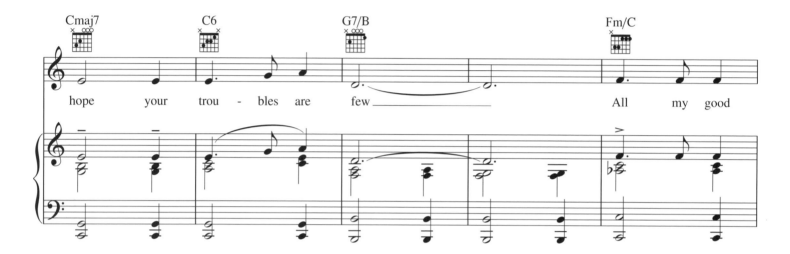

hope your trou-bles are few _____ All my good

wish-es go with you to-night— I've been in love like

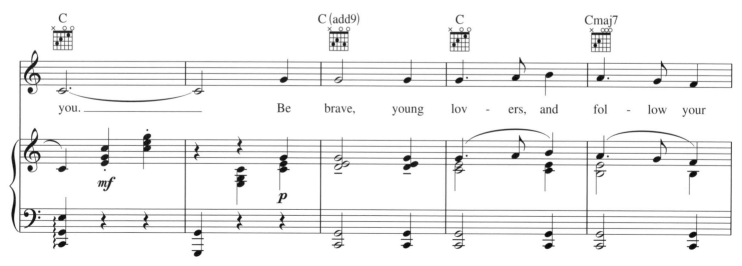

you. _____ Be brave, young lov-ers, and fol-low your

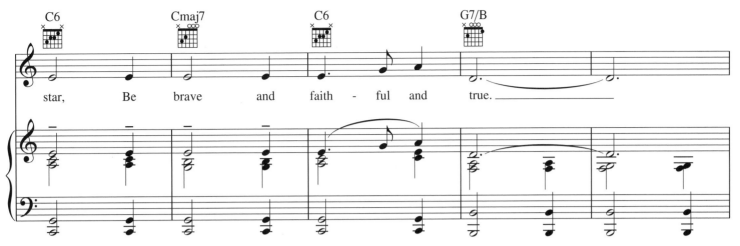

star, Be brave and faith - ful and true. _____

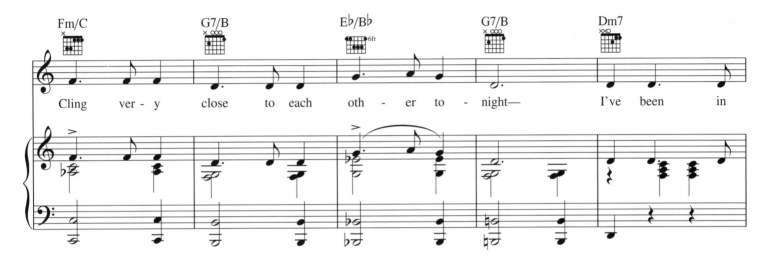

Cling ver - y close to each oth - er to - night— I've been in

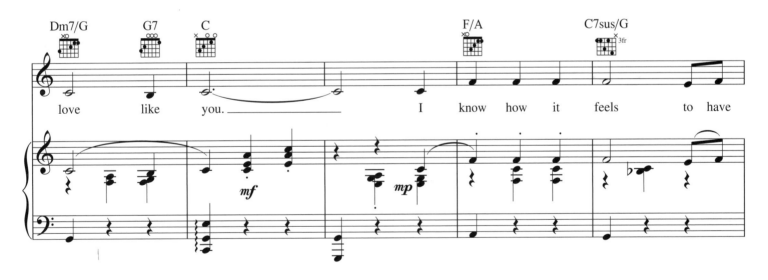

love like you. _____ I know how it feels to have

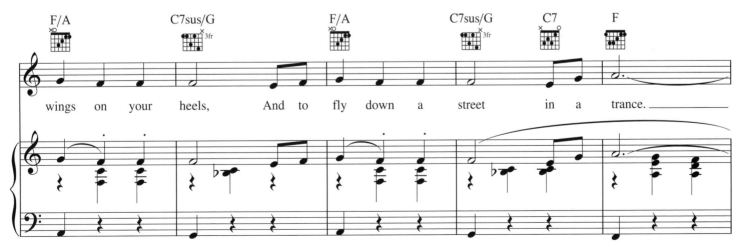

wings on your heels, And to fly down a street in a trance. _____

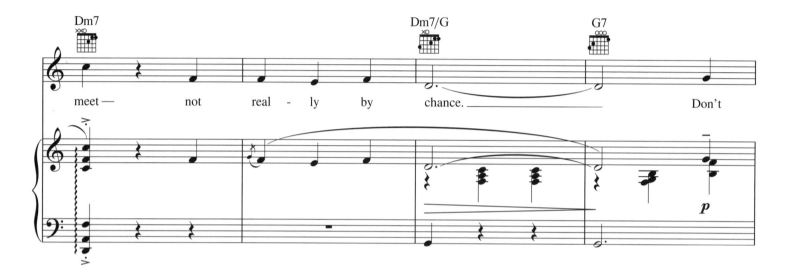

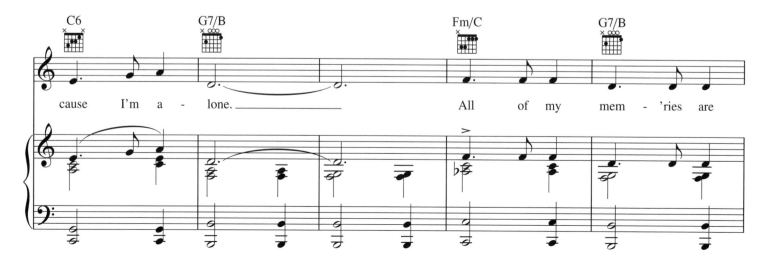

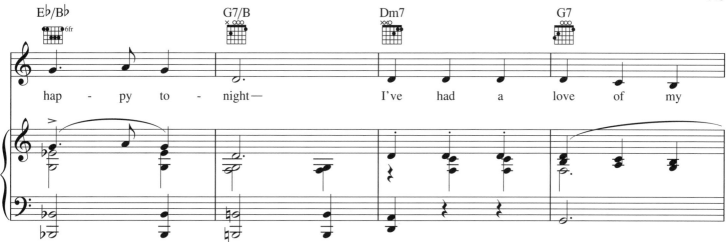

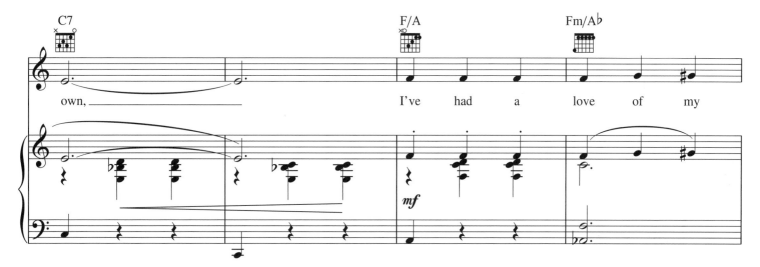

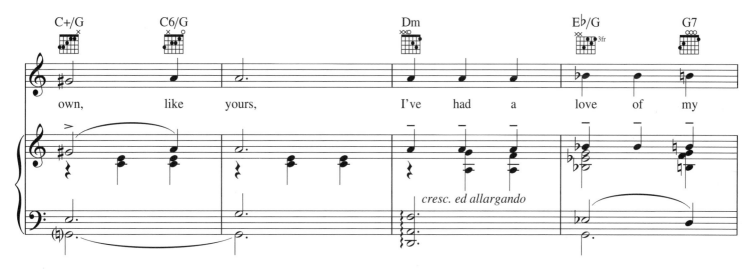

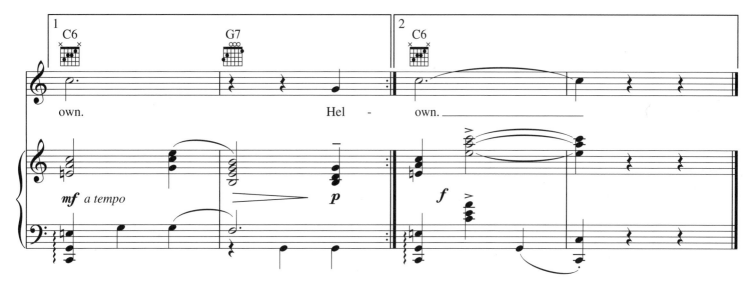

HOW HIGH THE MOON

from TWO FOR THE SHOW

Words by NANCY HAMILTON
Music by MORGAN LEWIS

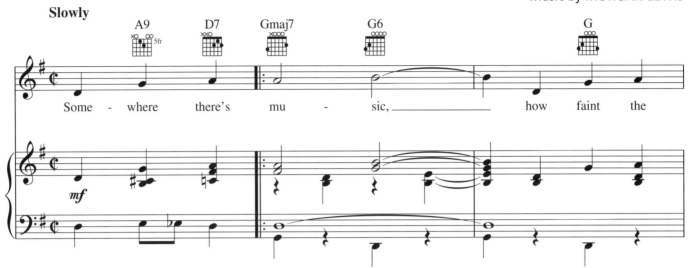

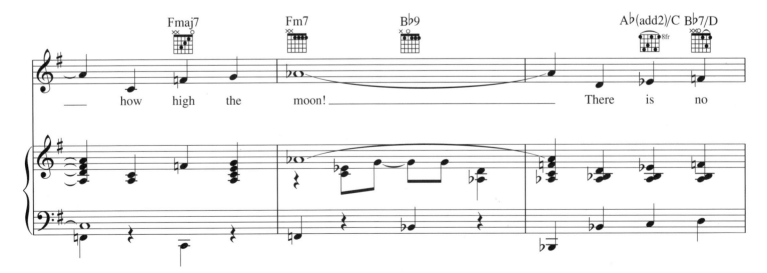

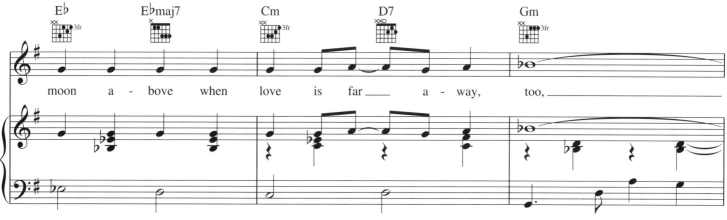

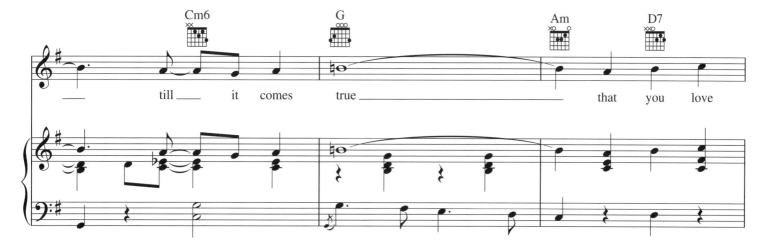

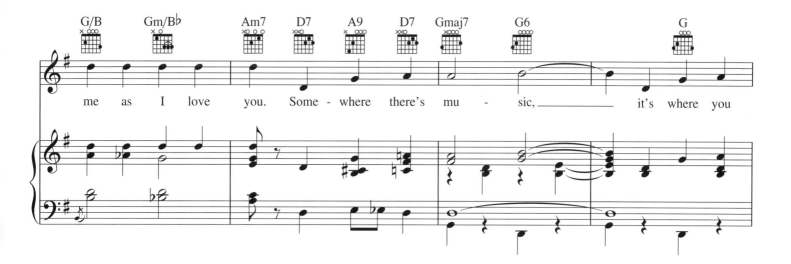

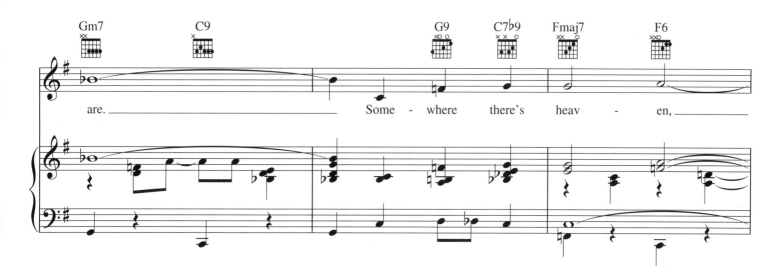

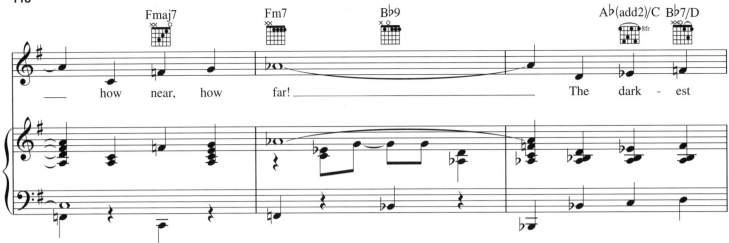

how near, how far! The dark-est

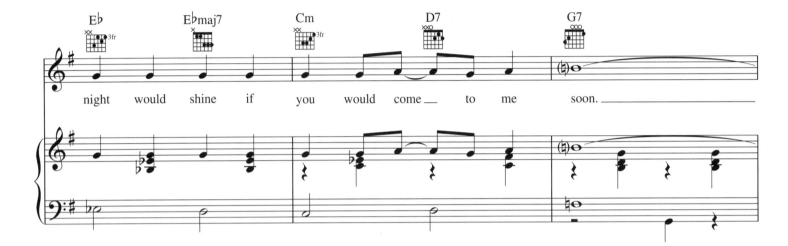

night would shine if you would come to me soon.

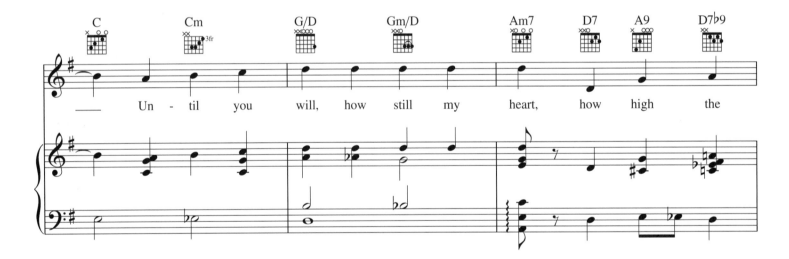

Un-til you will, how still my heart, how high the

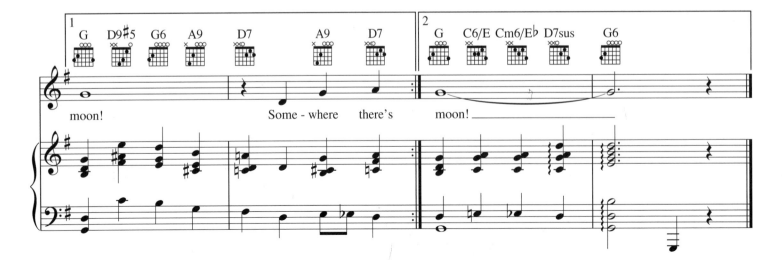

1. moon! Some-where there's
2. moon!

I CAN'T GET STARTED WITH YOU

from ZIEGFELD FOLLIES

Words by IRA GERSHWIN
Music by VERNON DUKE

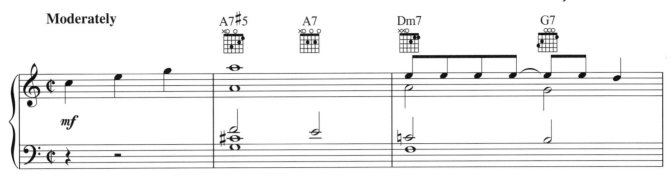

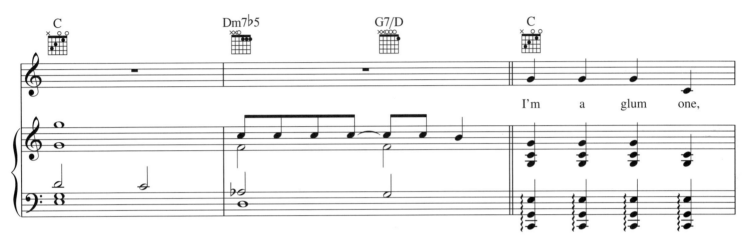

I'm a glum one,

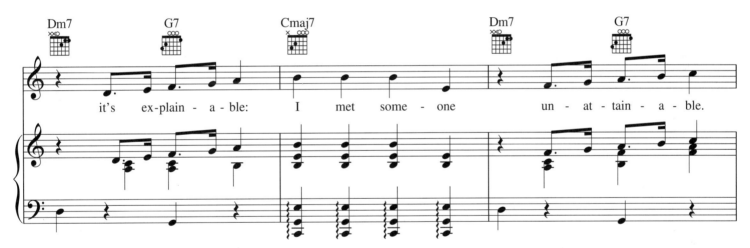

it's ex-plain-a-ble: I met some-one un-at-tain-a-ble.

Life's a bore, the world is my oy-ster no

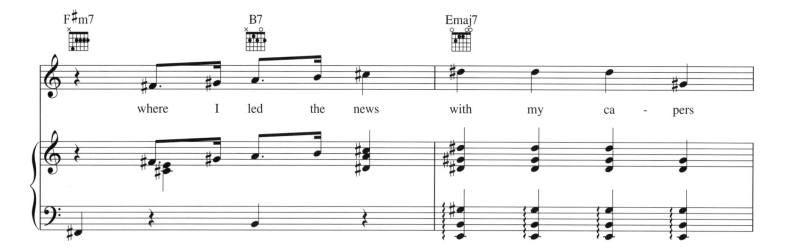

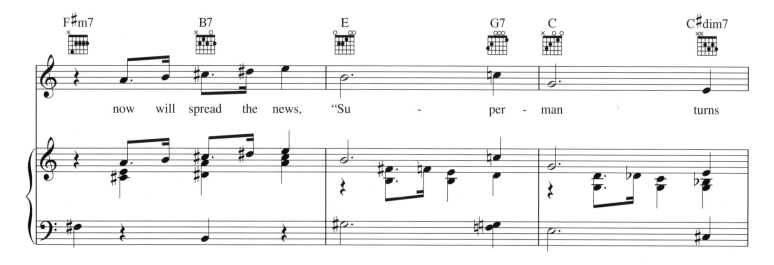

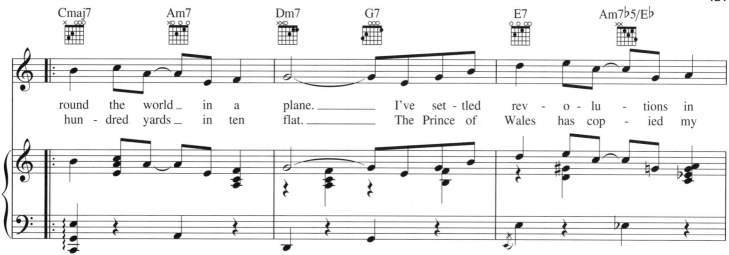

round the world_ in a plane._____ I've set-tled rev-o-lu-tions in
hun-dred yards_ in ten flat._____ The Prince of Wales has cop-ied my

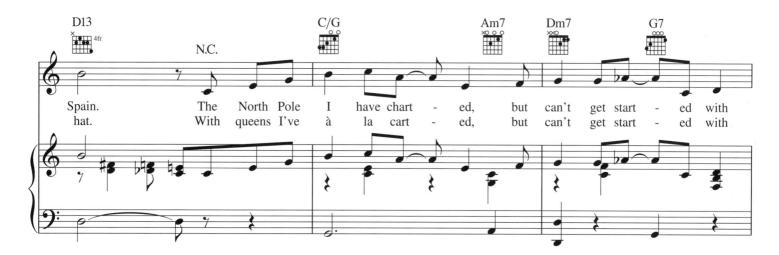

Spain._____ The North Pole I have chart-ed, but can't get start-ed with
hat._____ With queens I've à la cart-ed, but can't get start-ed with

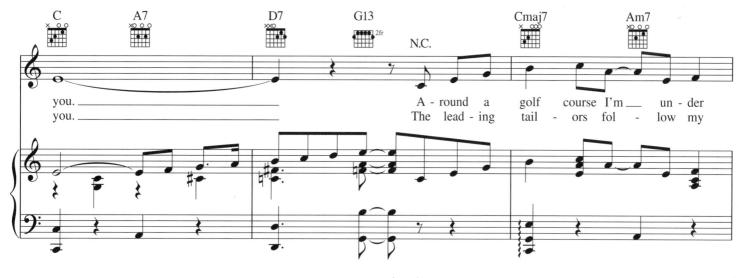

you._____ A-round a golf course I'm_ un-der
you._____ The lead-ing tail-ors fol-low my

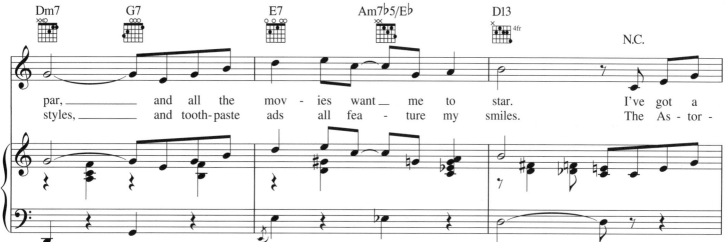

par,_____ and all the mov-ies want_ me to star._____ I've got a
styles,_____ and tooth-paste ads all fea-ture my smiles._____ The As-tor-

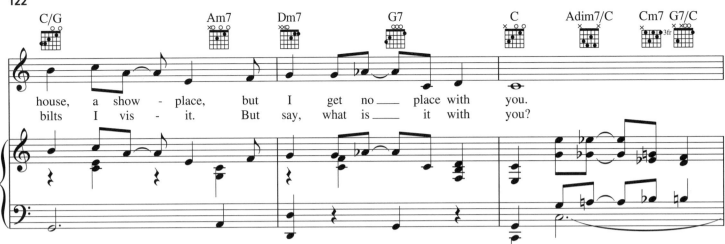

house, a show - place, but I get no ___ place with you.
bilts I vis - it. But say, what is ___ it with you?

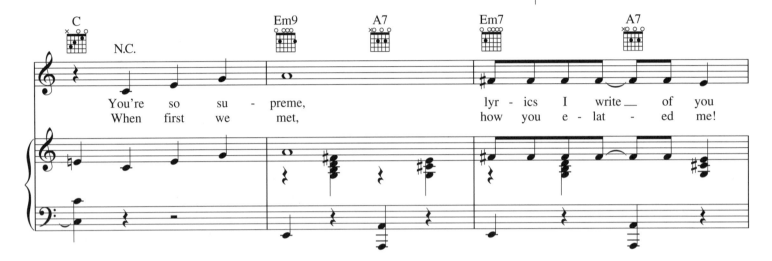

You're so su - preme, lyr - ics I write ___ of you
When first we met, how you e - lat - ed me!

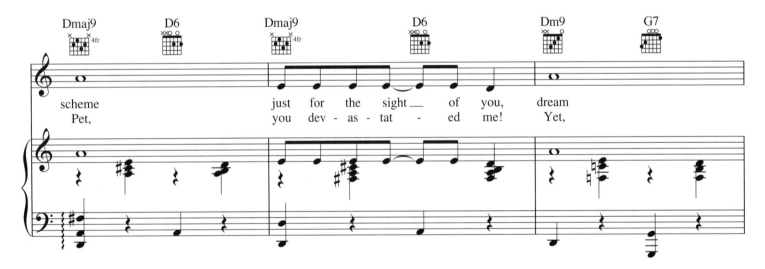

scheme just for the sight ___ of you, dream
Pet, you dev - as - tat - ed me! Yet,

both day and night ___ of you. And what good does it do? In nine - teen
now you've de - flat - ed me till you're my Wa - ter - loo. I've sold my

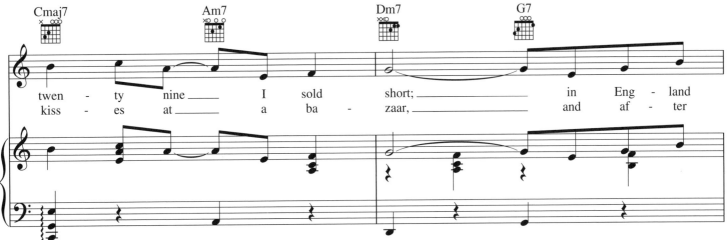

twen - ty nine _____ I sold short; _____ in Eng - land
kiss - es at _____ I a ba - zaar, _____ and af - ter

I'm pre - sent - ed at court. But you've got me down-heart - ed 'cause I
me they've named ___ a ci - gar. But late - ly how I've smart - ed, 'cause I

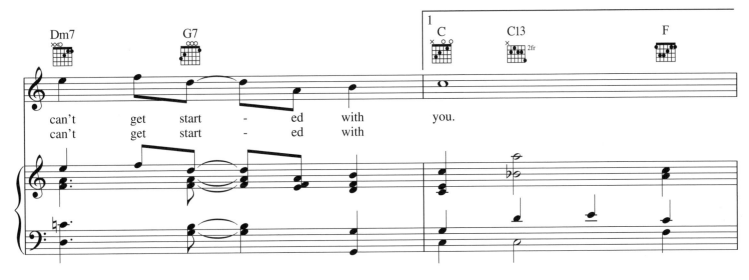

can't get start - ed with you.
can't get start - ed with

1

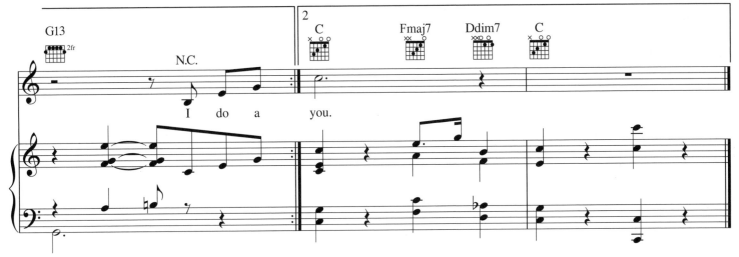

2

I do a you.

HOW INSENSITIVE
(Insensatez)

Music by ANTONIO CARLOS JOBIM
Original Words by VINICIUS DE MORAES
English Words by NORMAN GIMBEL

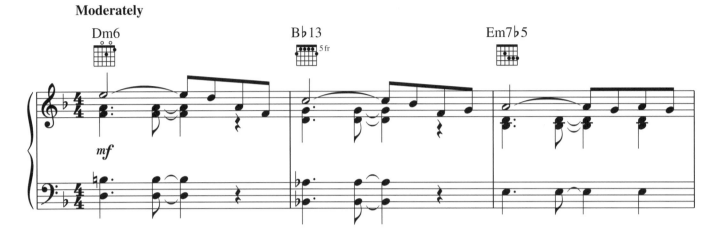

How _____ in - sen - si - tive _____
Now, _____ {he's / she's} gone _ a - way _____

_ I must _ have seemed _____ when he told me that _ {he / she} loved _ me. _____
_ and I'm a - lone _____ with the mem-'ry of _ {his / her} last _ look. _____

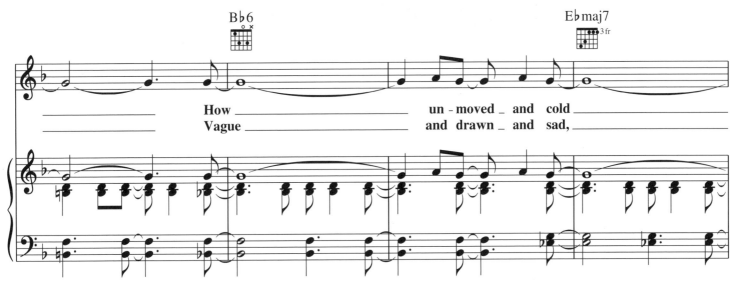

How _____ un-moved ___ and cold _____
Vague _____ and drawn ___ and sad, _____

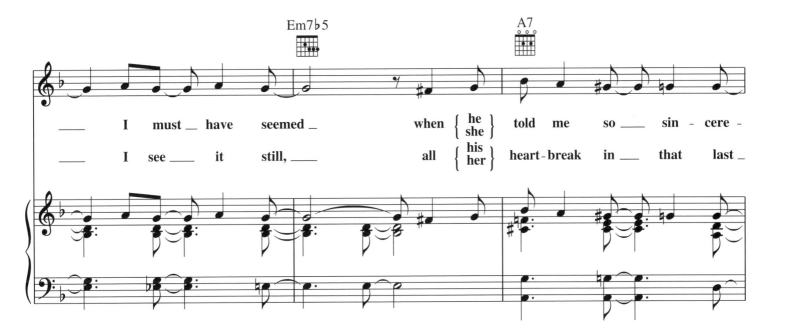

___ I must ___ have seemed ___ when { he / she } told me so ___ sin - cere -
___ I see ___ it still, ___ all { his / her } heart-break in ___ that last ___

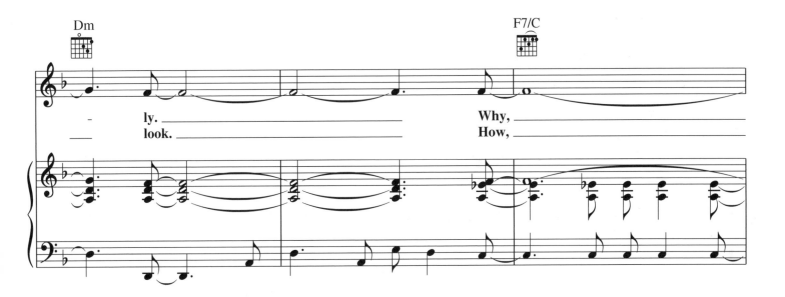

- ly. _____ Why, _____
___ look. _____ How, _____

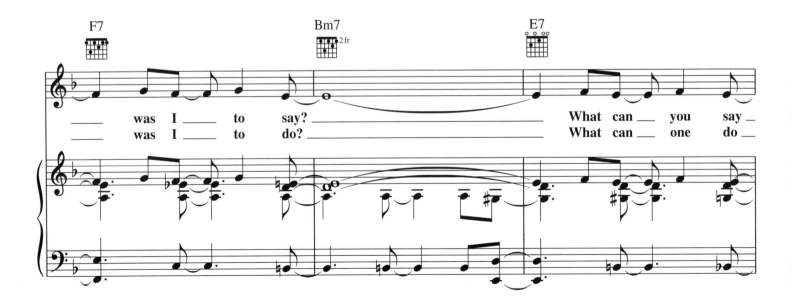

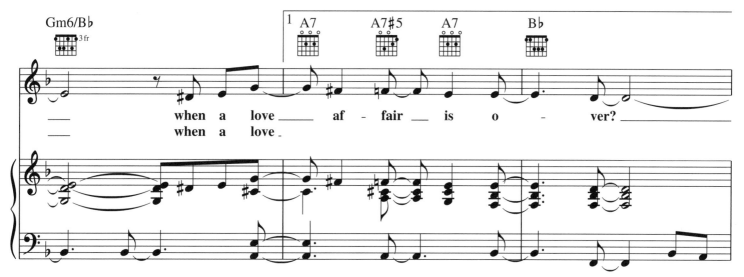

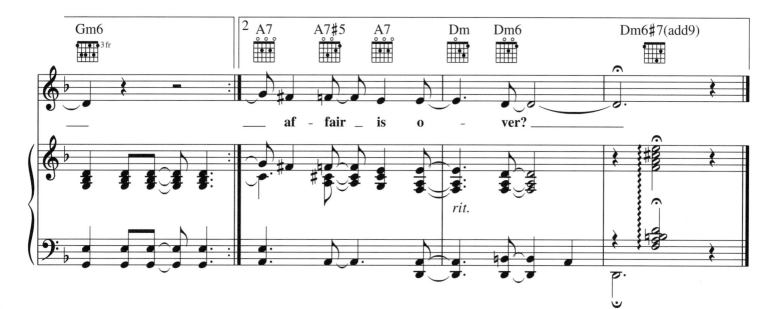

Portuguese Lyrics

A insensatez
Que você fez
Coração mais sem cuidado
Fez chorar de dôr
O seu amôr
Um amôr tão delicado
Ah! Porque você
Foi fraco assim
Assim tão desalmado
Ah! Meu coração
Que nunca amou
Não merece ser amado
Vai meu coração
Ouve a razão
Usa só sinceridade
Quem semeia vento
Diz a razão
Colhe tempestade
Vai meu coração
Pede perdão
Perdão apaixonado
Vai porque
Quem não
Pede perdão
Não é nunca perdoado.

I COULD WRITE A BOOK
from PAL JOEY

Words by LORENZ HART
Music by RICHARD RODGERS

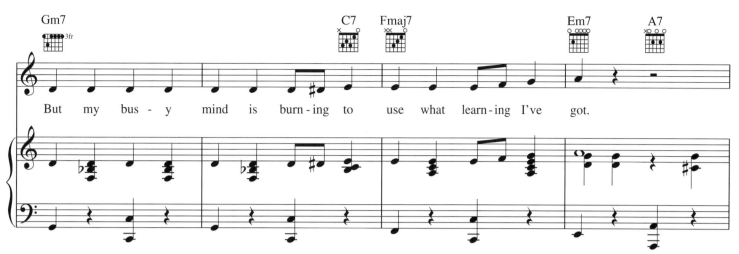

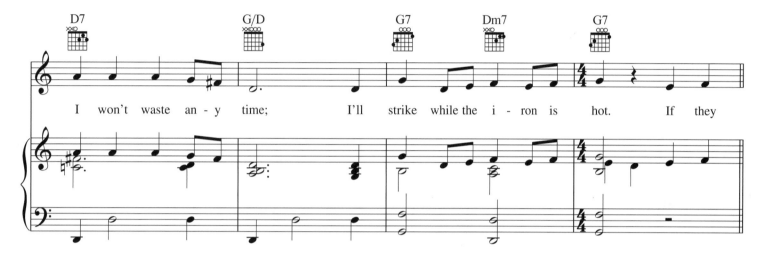

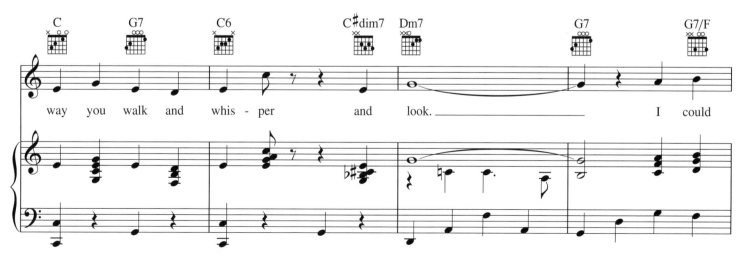

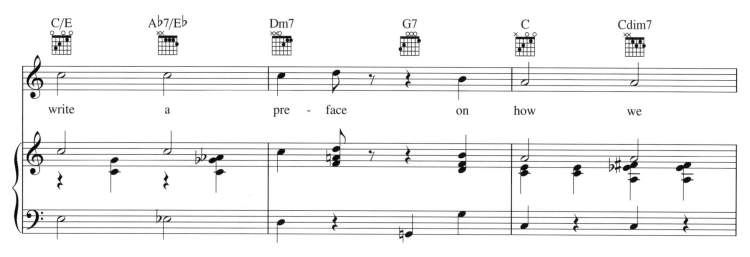

write a pre - face on how we

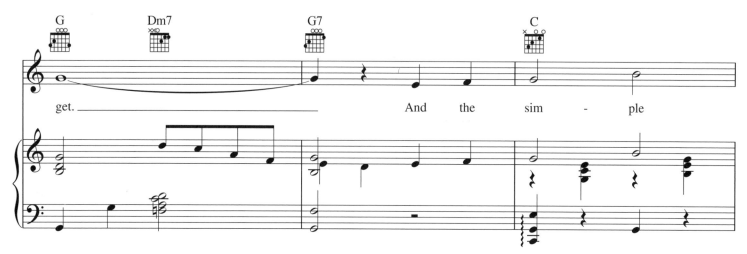

met so the world would nev - er for -

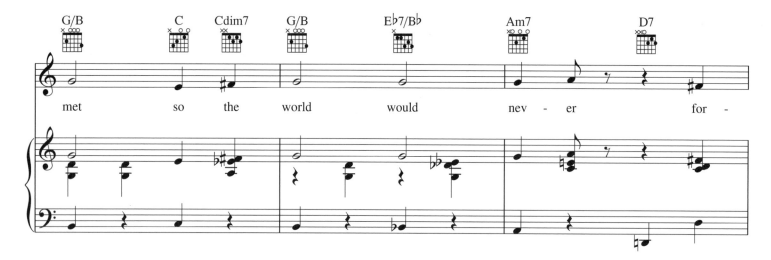

get. _____ And the sim - ple

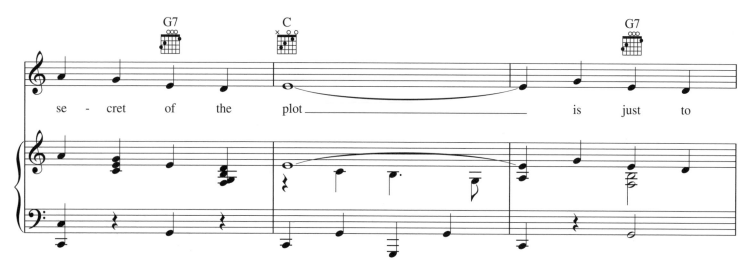

se - cret of the plot _____ is just to

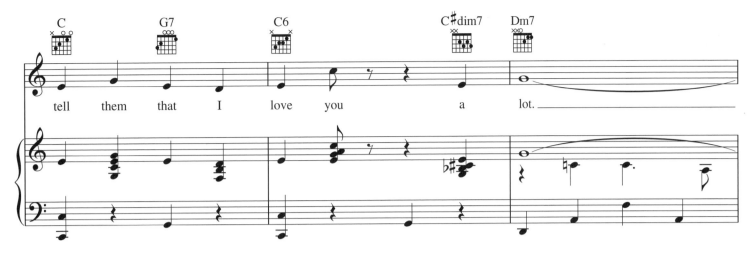

tell them that I love you a lot._____

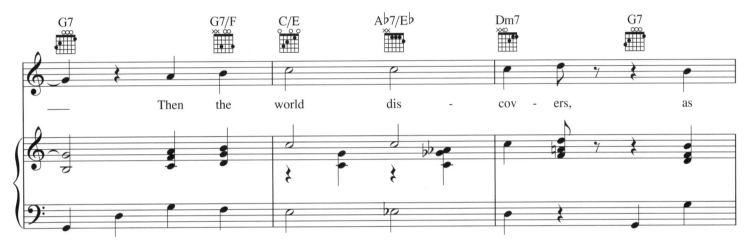

____ Then the world dis - cov - ers, as

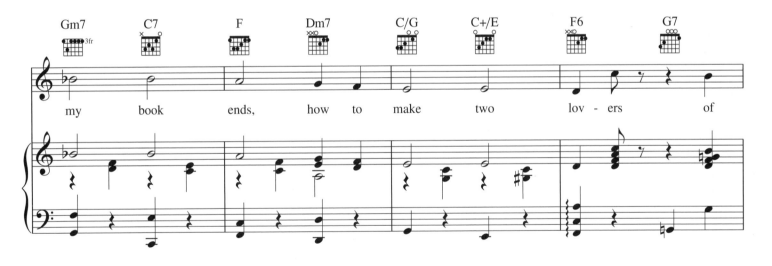

my book ends, how to make two lov - ers of

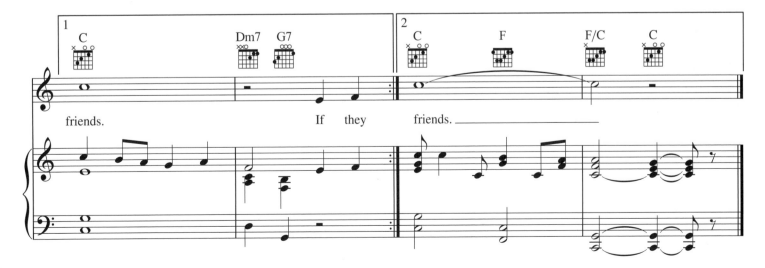

1
friends.   If they   friends._____

2

I WON'T DANCE

from ROBERTA

Words and Music by JIMMY McHUGH, DOROTHY FIELDS,
JEROME KERN, OSCAR HAMMERSTEIN II and OTTO HARBACH

I'LL TAKE ROMANCE

Lyrics by OSCAR HAMMERSTEIN II
Music by BEN OAKLAND

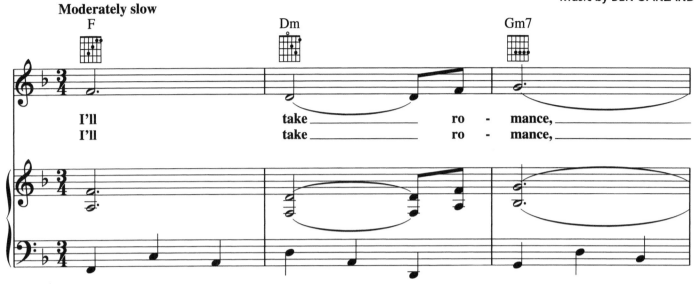

I'll take _____ ro - mance, _____
I'll take _____ ro - mance, _____

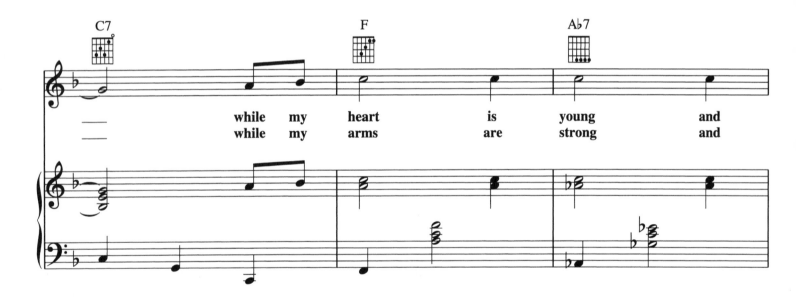

while my heart is young and
while my arms are strong and

ea - ger to fly.
ea - ger for you.

I'll give my
I'll give my

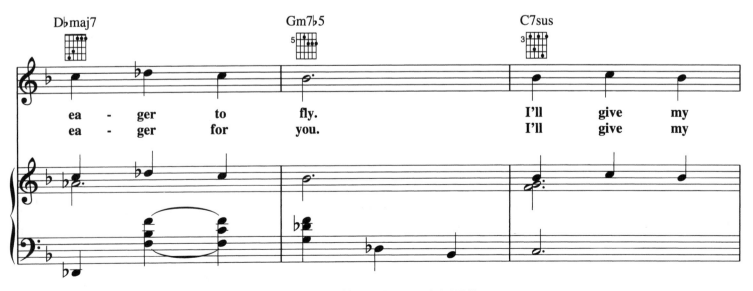

I'M BEGINNING TO SEE THE LIGHT

Words and Music by DON GEORGE, JOHNNY HODGES,
DUKE ELLINGTON and HARRY JAMES

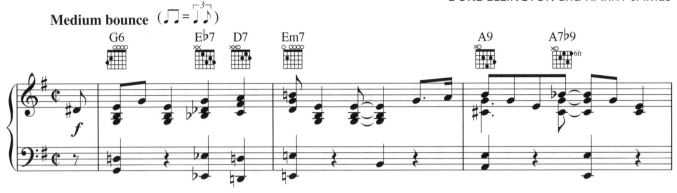

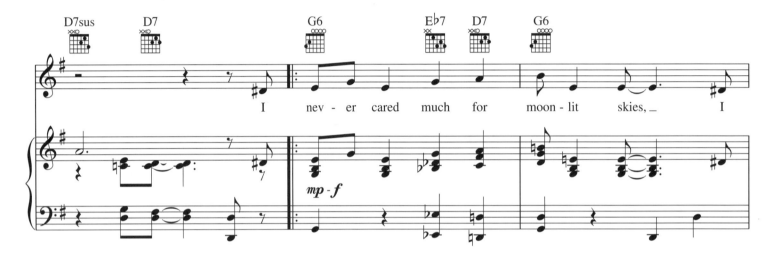

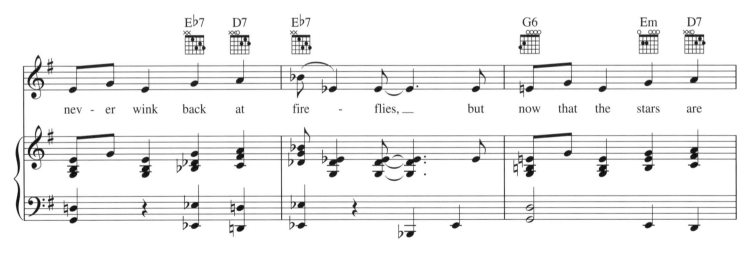

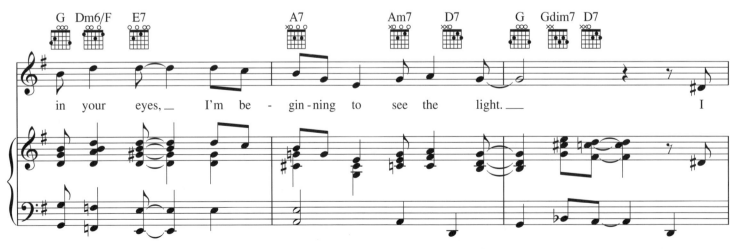

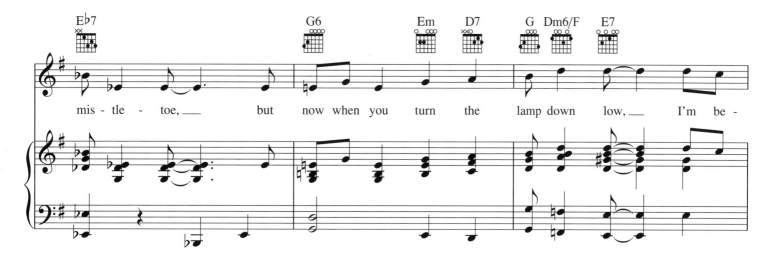

never went in for af-ter-glow __ or can-dle-light on the

mis-tle - toe, __ but now when you turn the lamp down low, __ I'm be -

gin - ning to see the light. ____ Used to ram - ble

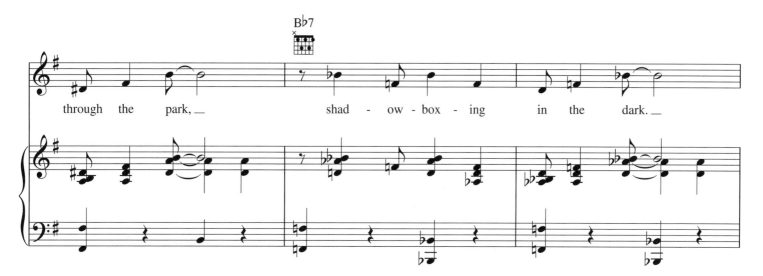

through the park, __ shad - ow - box - ing in the dark. __

Then you came and caused a spark __ that's a four a - larm fire __ now.

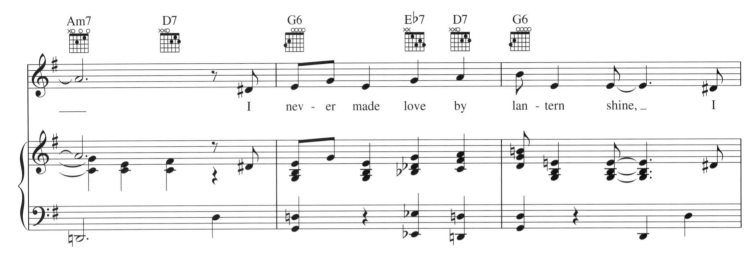

__ I nev - er made love by lan - tern shine, __ I

nev - er saw rain - bows in my wine, __ but now that your lips are

burn - ing mine, __ I'm be - gin - ning to see the light. __ I __

8vb

I'VE GOT YOU UNDER MY SKIN
from BORN TO DANCE

Words and Music by
COLE PORTER

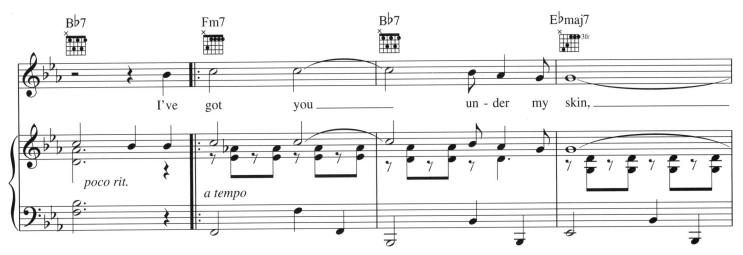

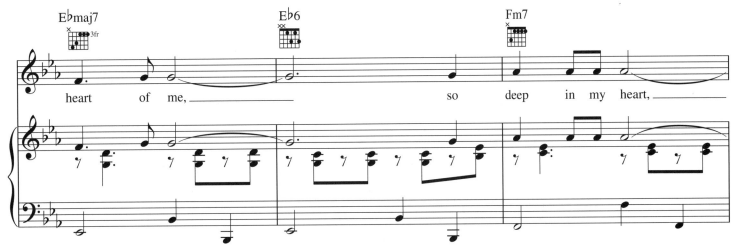

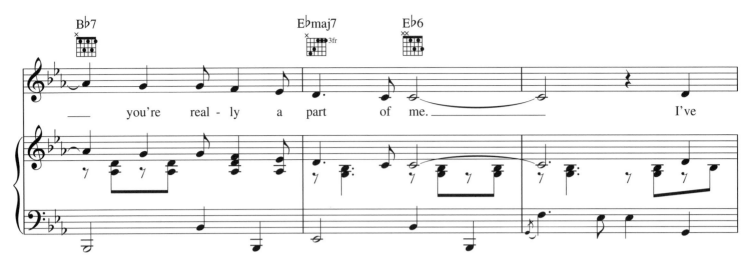

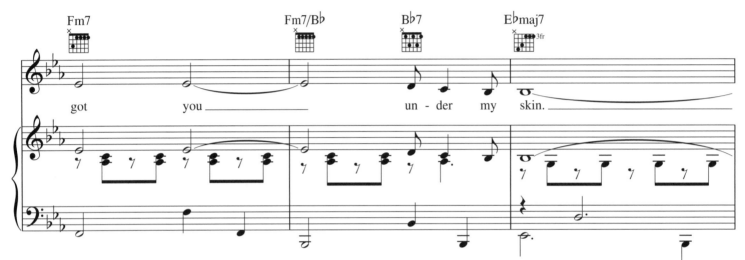

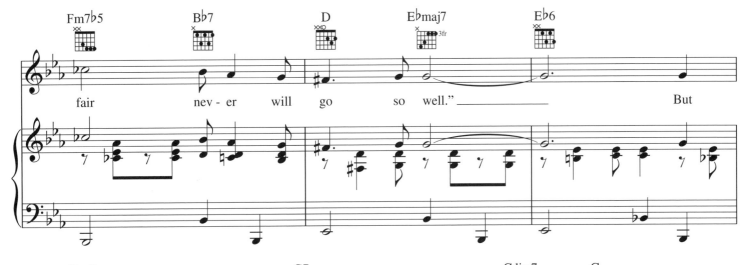

fair nev - er will go so well." _____ But

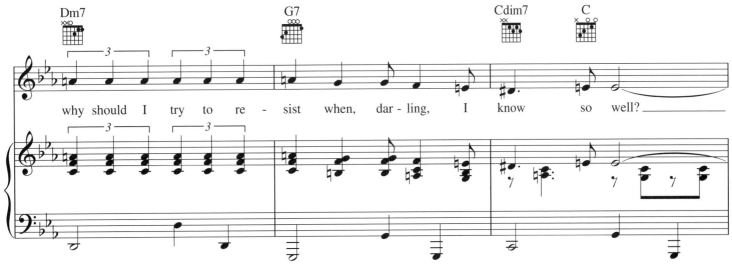

why should I try to re - sist when, dar - ling, I know so well? _____

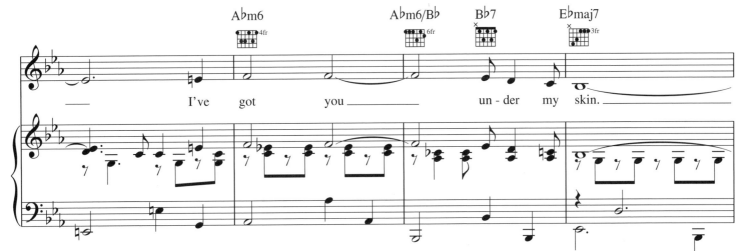

I've got you _____ un - der my skin. _____

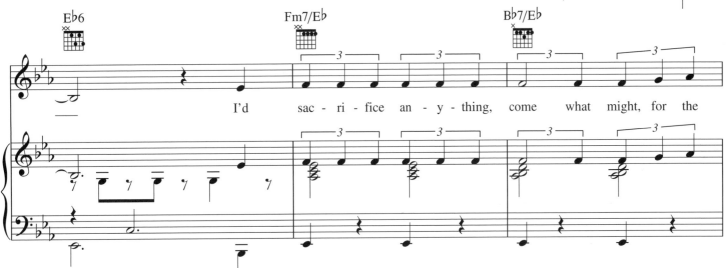

I'd sac - ri - fice an - y - thing, come what might, for the

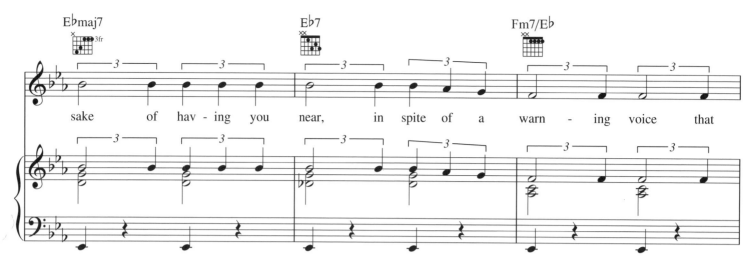

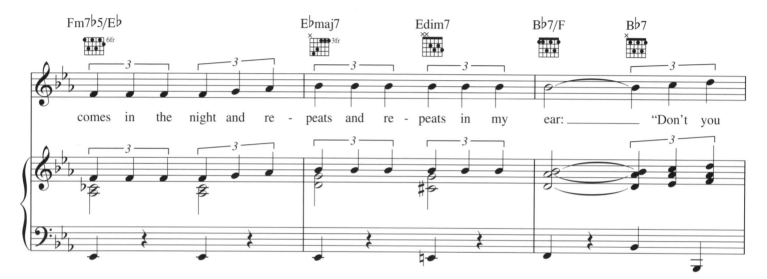

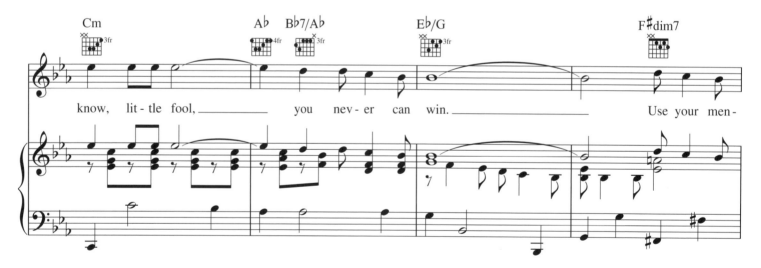

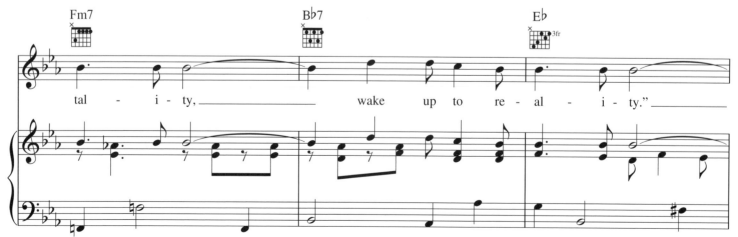

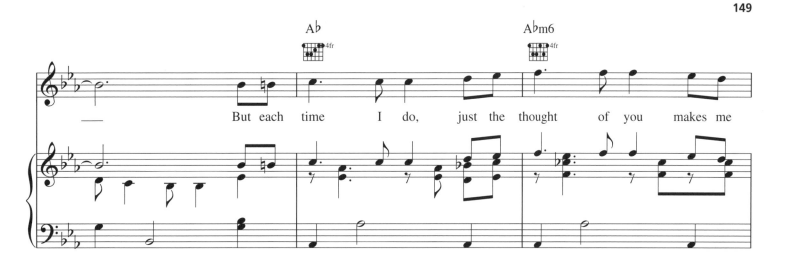

But each time I do, just the thought of you makes me

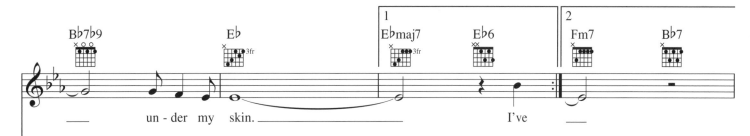

stop be-fore I be-gin, 'cause I've got you

rit.

a tempo

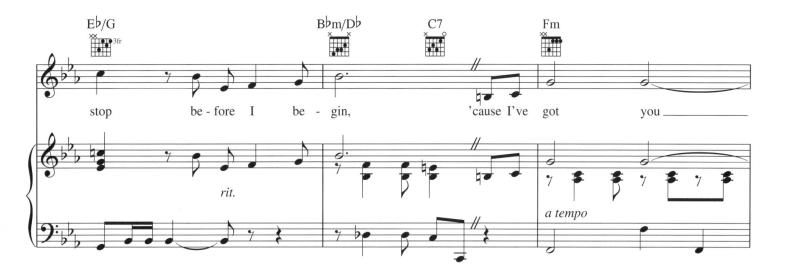

un-der my skin. I've

poco rall.

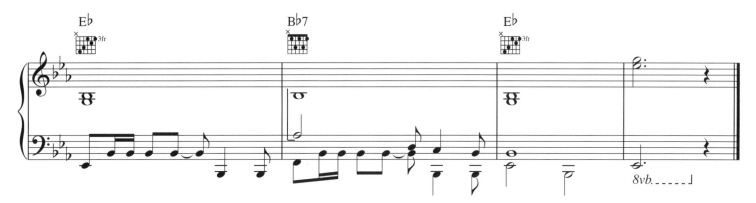

8vb.

IN A MELLOW TONE

Words by MILT GABLER
Music by DUKE ELLINGTON

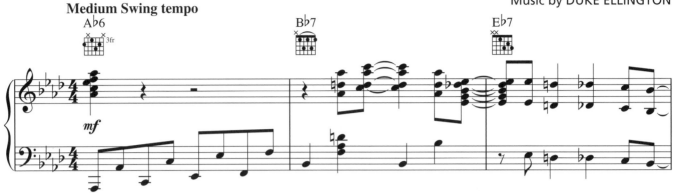

Medium Swing tempo

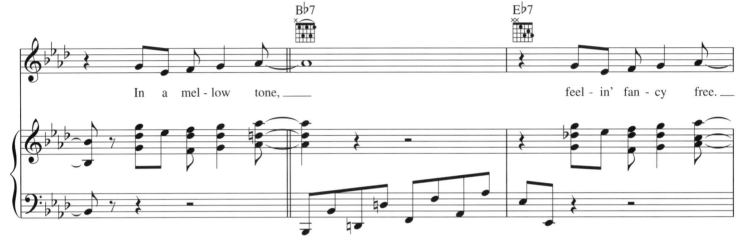

In a mel-low tone, _____ feel-in' fan-cy free. _____

_____ And I'm not a-lone, _____

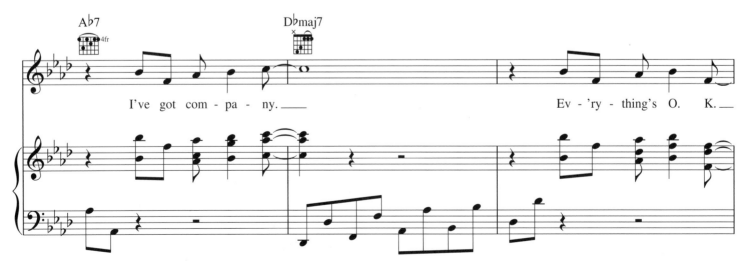

I've got com-pa-ny. _____ Ev-'ry-thing's O. K. _____

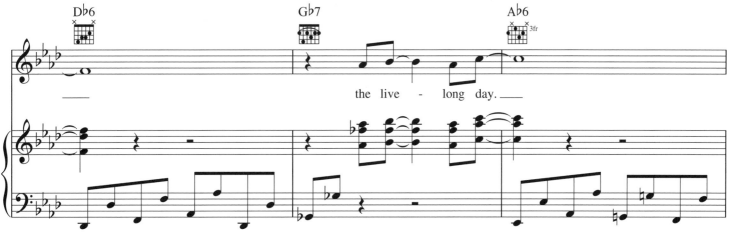

the live - long day. ___

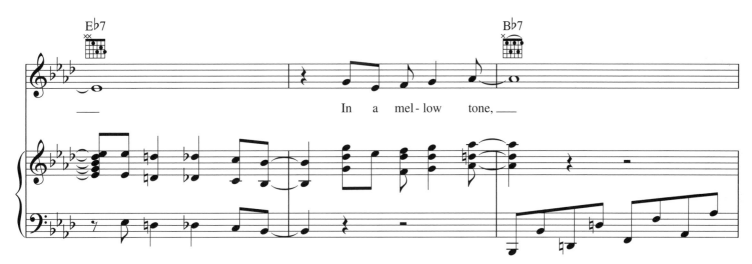

With this mel - low song ___ I can't ___ go wrong. ___

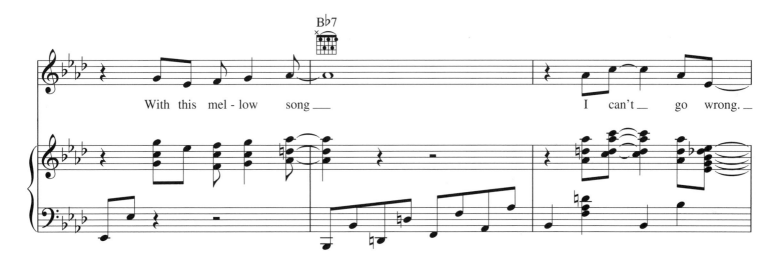

In a mel - low tone, ___

that's the way to live. ___ If you mope and groan, ___

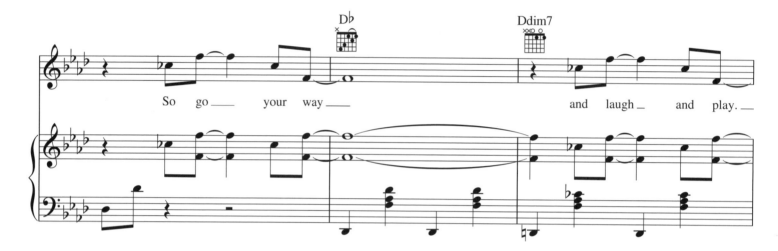

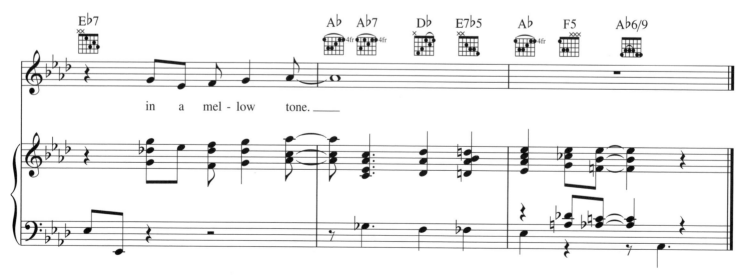

IT MIGHT AS WELL BE SPRING

from STATE FAIR

Lyrics by OSCAR HAMMERSTEIN II
Music by RICHARD RODGERS

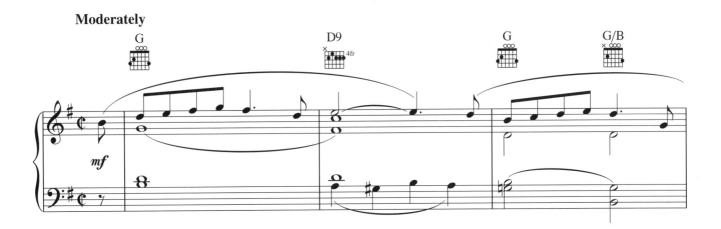

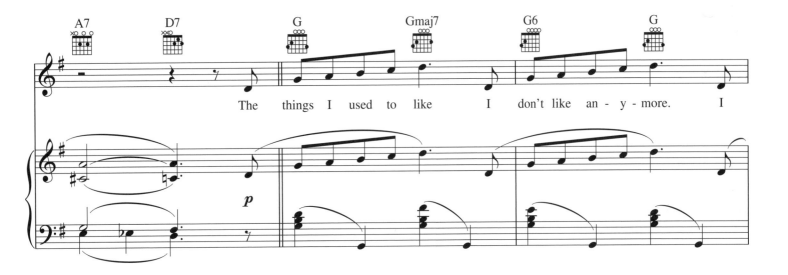

The things I used to like I don't like an-y-more. I

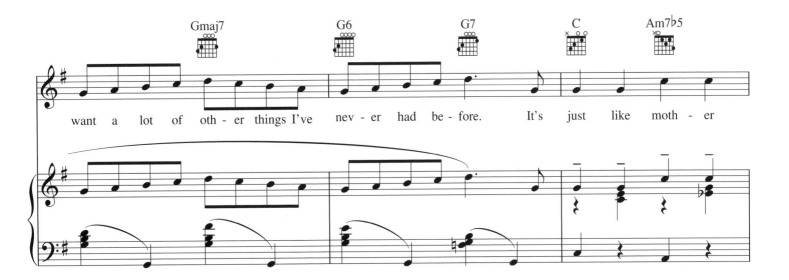

want a lot of oth-er things I've nev-er had be-fore. It's just like moth-er

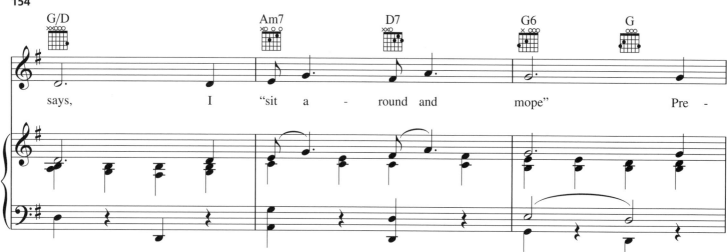

says, I "sit a - round and mope" Pre -

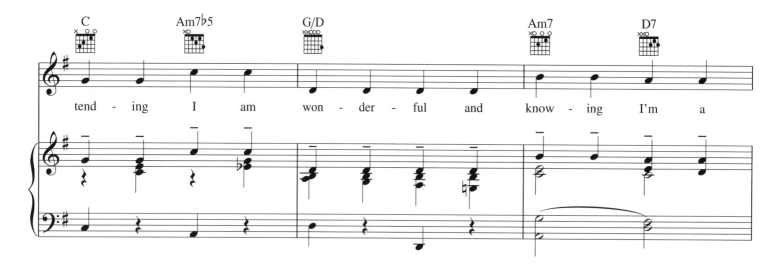

tend - ing I am won - der - ful and know - ing I'm a

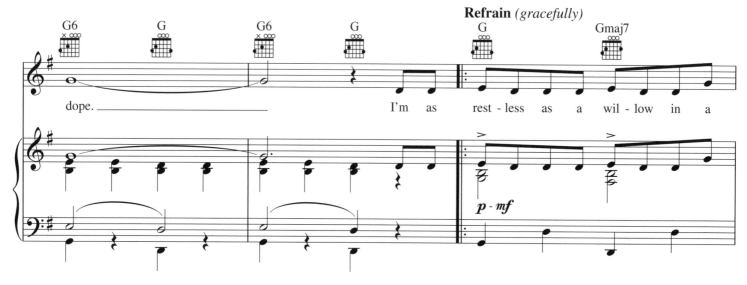

Refrain (gracefully)

dope. _____ I'm as rest - less as a wil - low in a

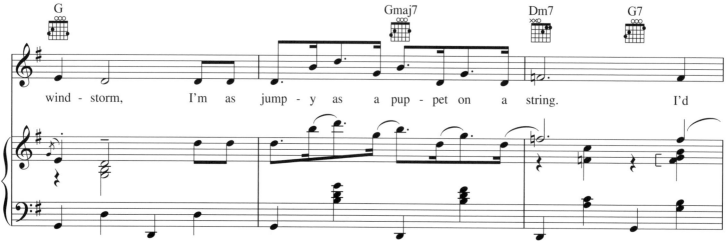

wind - storm, I'm as jump - y as a pup - pet on a string. I'd

say that I had spring fe - ver, But I know it is - n't

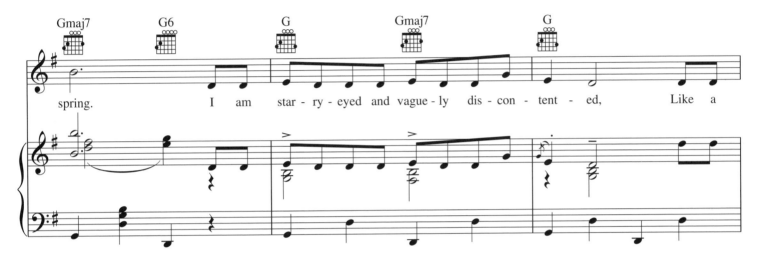

spring. I am star - ry - eyed and vague - ly dis - con - tent - ed, Like a

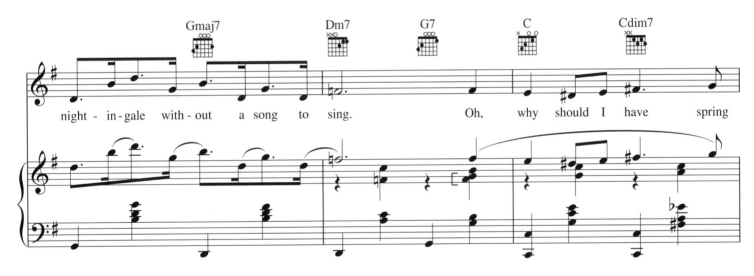

night - in - gale with - out a song to sing. Oh, why should I have spring

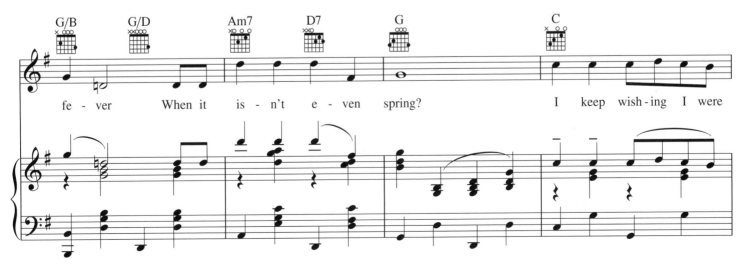

fe - ver When it is - n't e - ven spring? I keep wish - ing I were

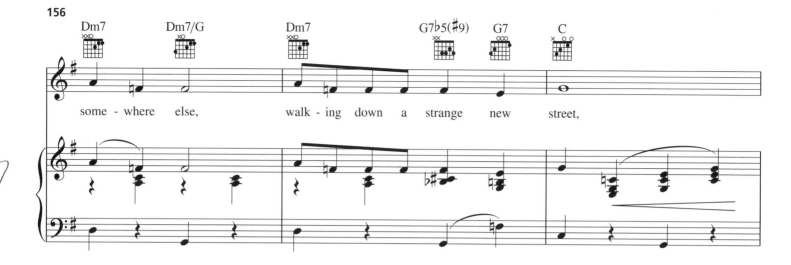

some-where else, walk-ing down a strange new street,

Hear-ing words that I have nev-er heard from a {man} {girl} I've yet to meet. I'm as

bus-y as a spi-der spin-ning day-dreams, I'm as gid-dy as a ba-by on a

swing. I have-n't seen a cro-cus or a rose-bud, or a

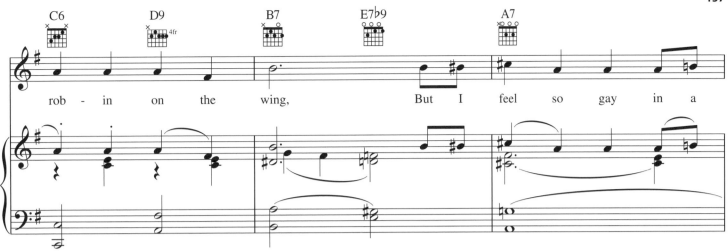

rob - in on the wing, But I feel so gay in a

mel - an - cho - ly way that it might as well be spring. It

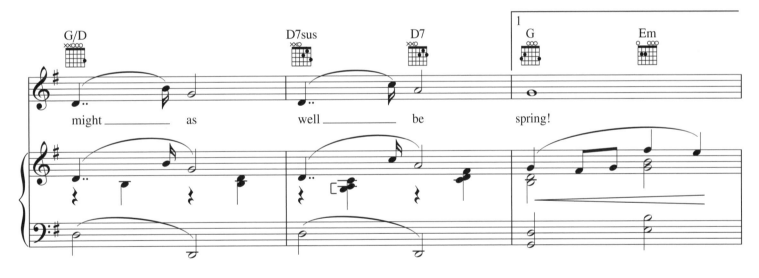

might _____ as well _____ be spring!

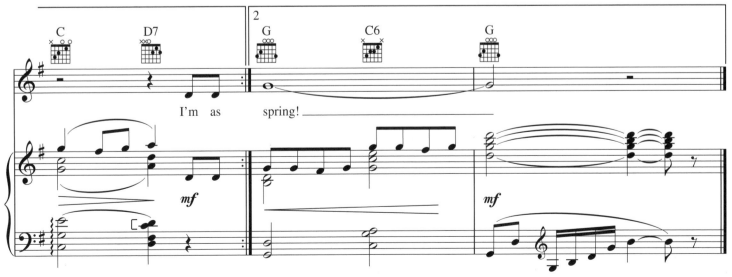

I'm as spring! _____

JELLY ROLL BLUES

By FERDINAND "JELLY ROLL" MORTON

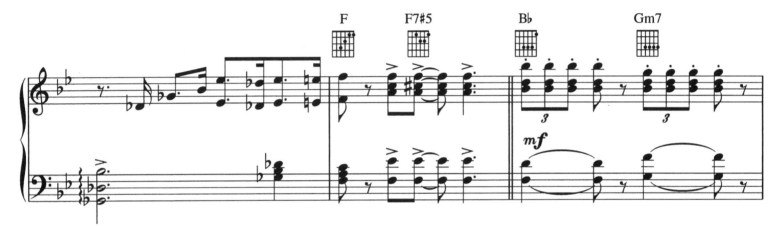

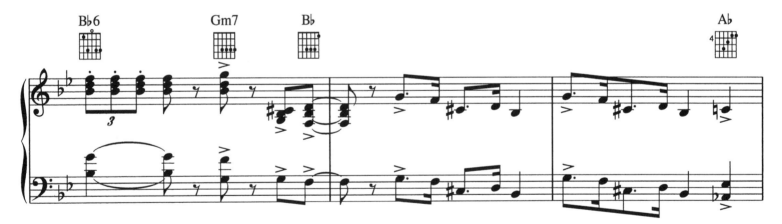

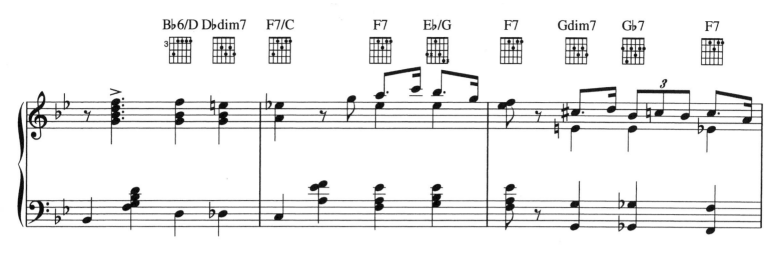

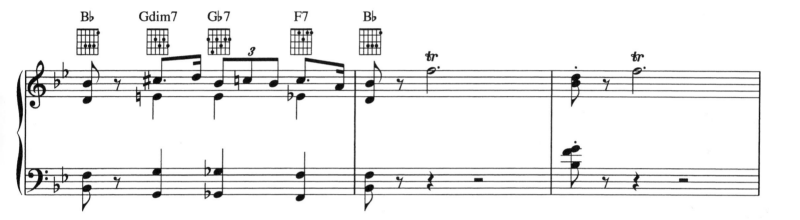

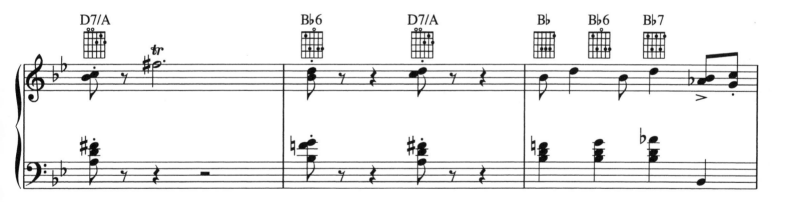

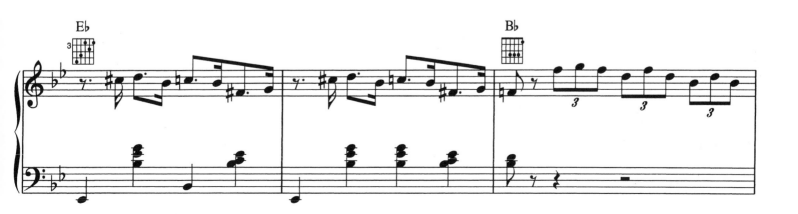

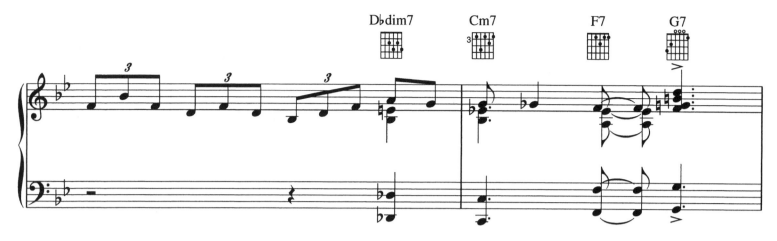

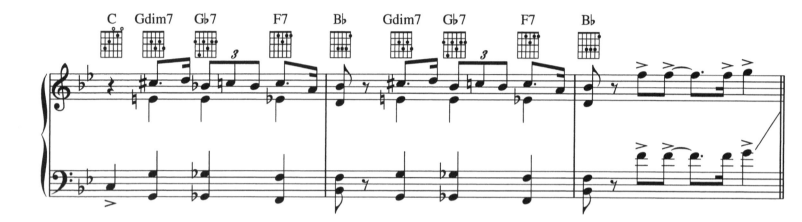

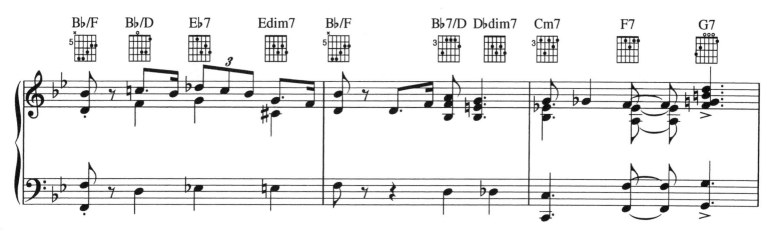

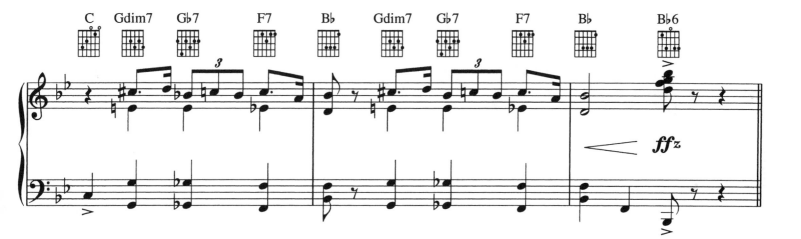

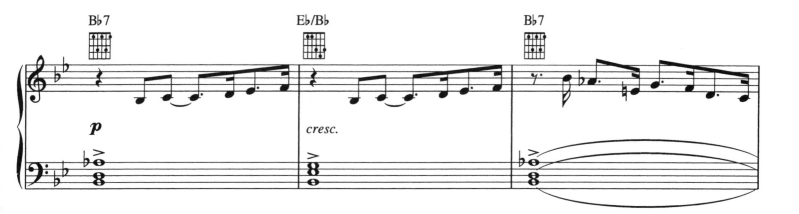

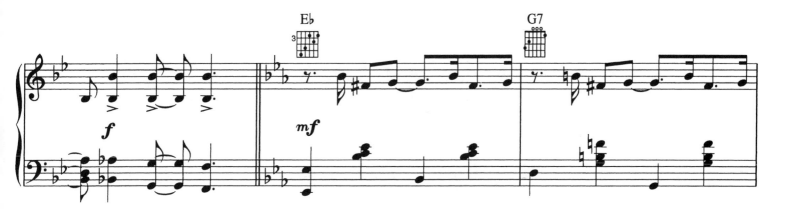

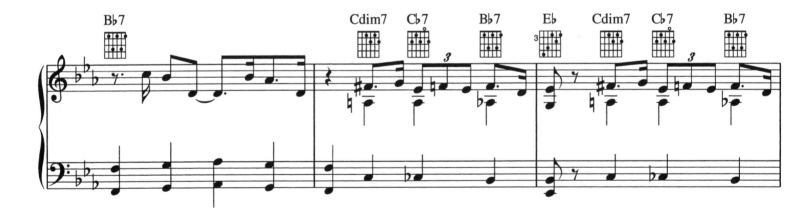

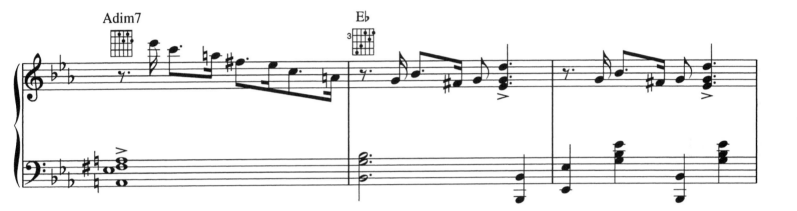

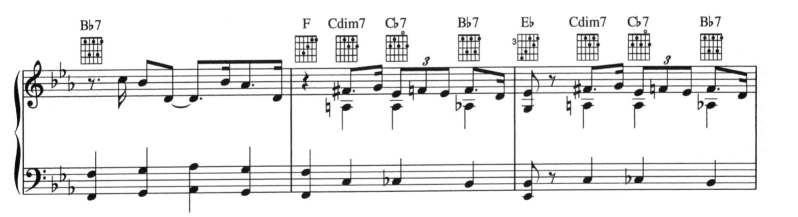

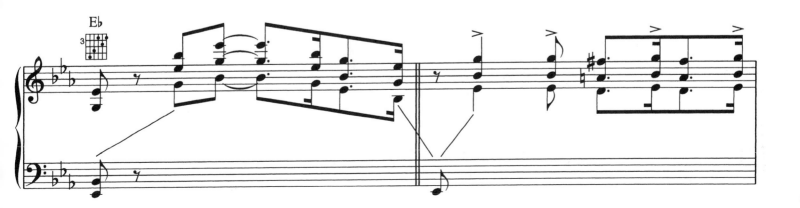

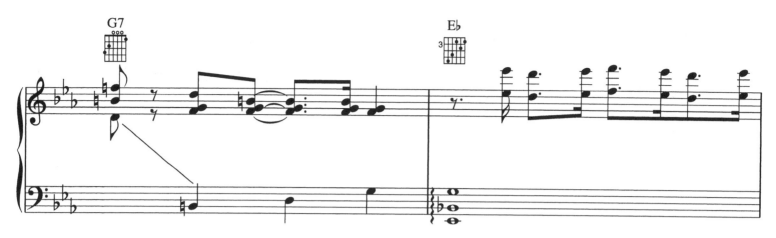

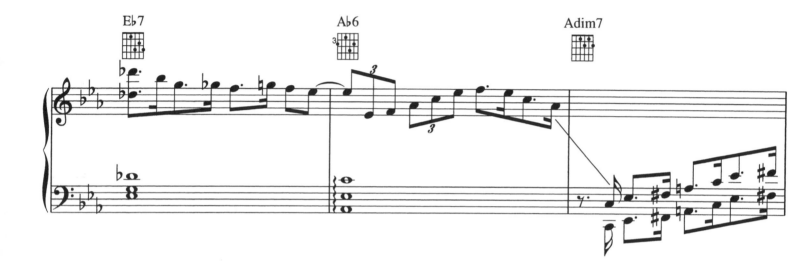

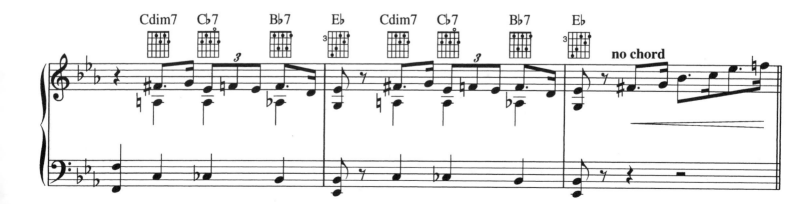

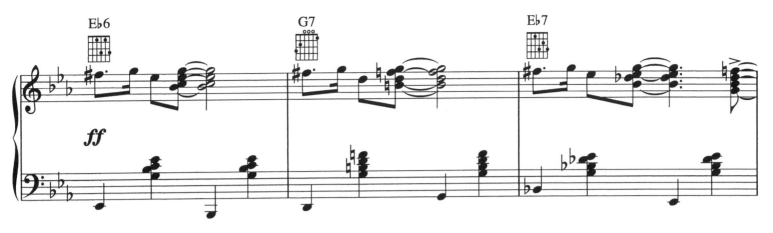

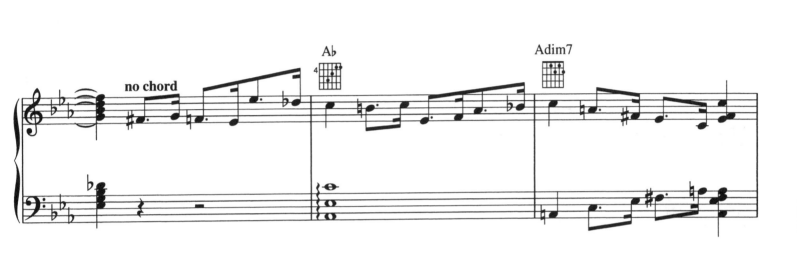

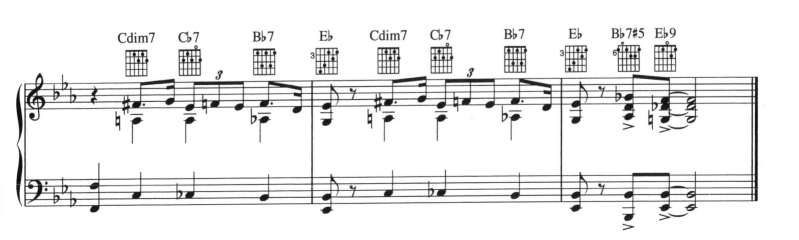

JUST IN TIME

from BELLS ARE RINGING

Words by BETTY COMDEN and ADOLPH GREEN
Music by JULE STYNE

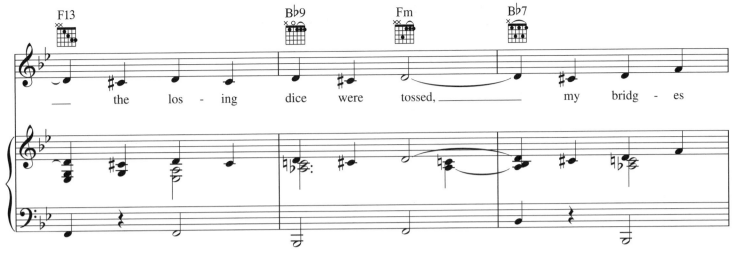

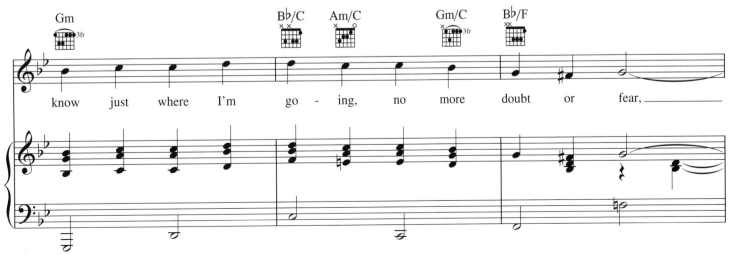

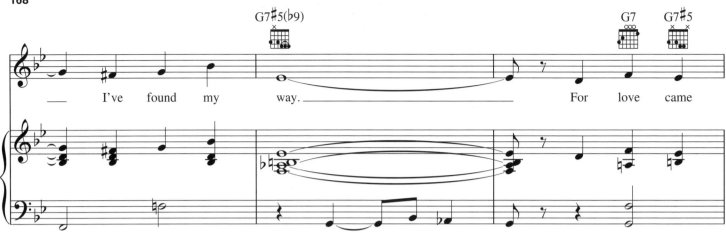

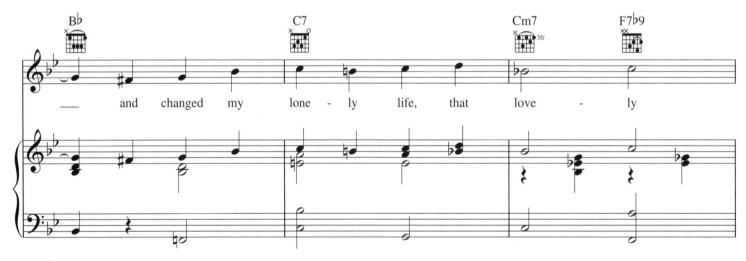

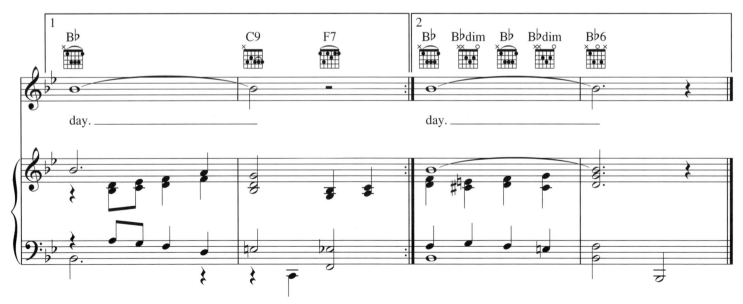

LA FIESTA

By CHICK COREA

Moderately, in 1

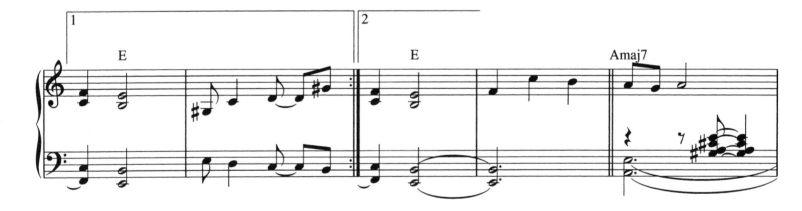

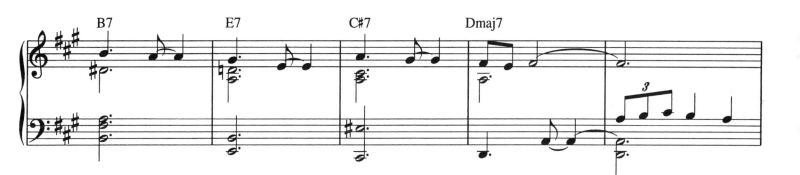

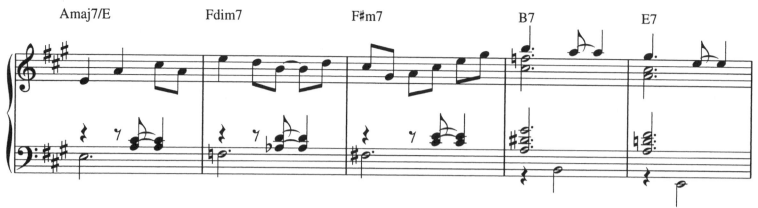

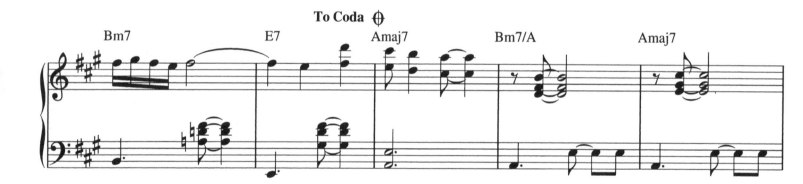

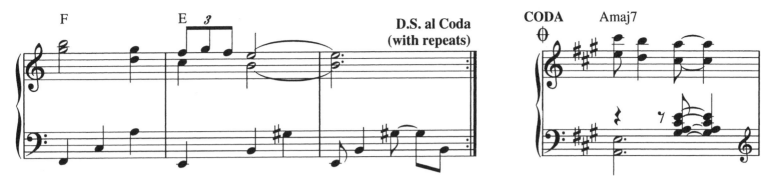

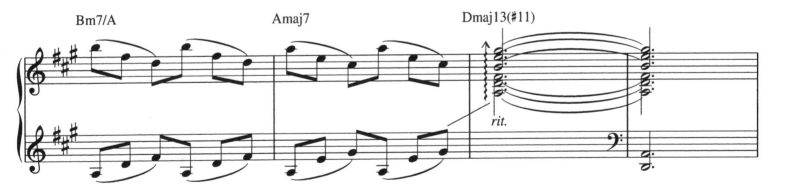

LADY SINGS THE BLUES

Words and Music by HERBERT NICHOLS
and BILLIE HOLIDAY

Slow Blues

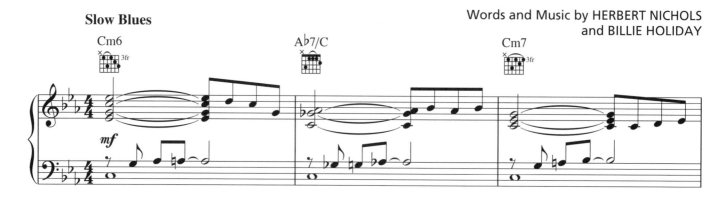

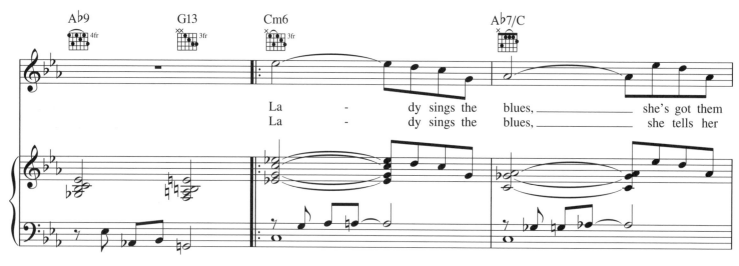

La - dy sings the blues, _____ she's got them
La - dy sings the blues, _____ she tells her

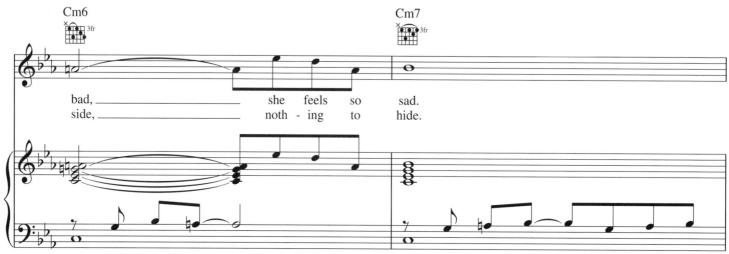

bad, _____ she feels so sad.
side, _____ noth - ing to hide.

Wants _____ the world to know _____ what the blues
Now _____ the world will know _____ just what the

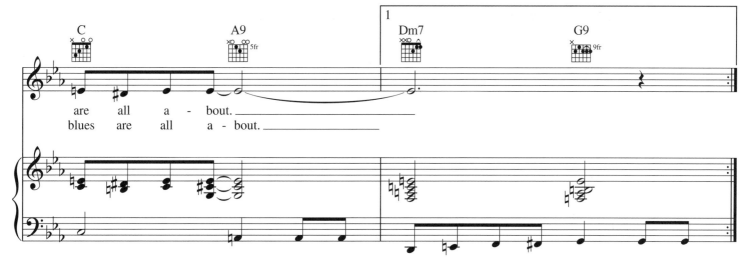

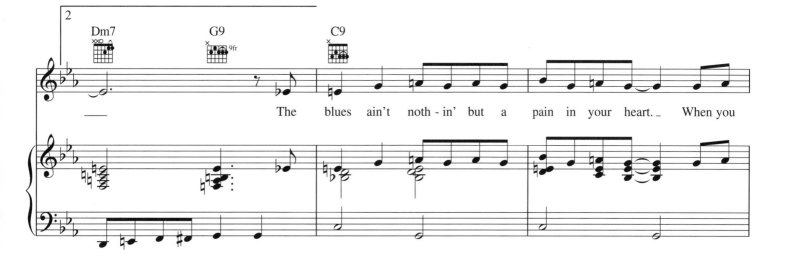

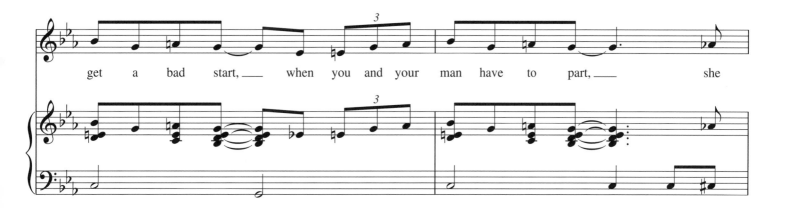

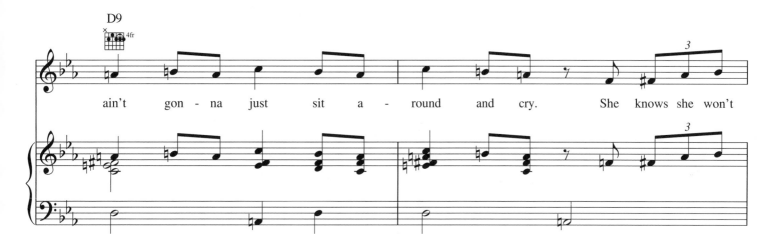

die _____ be - cause she loves him. _____

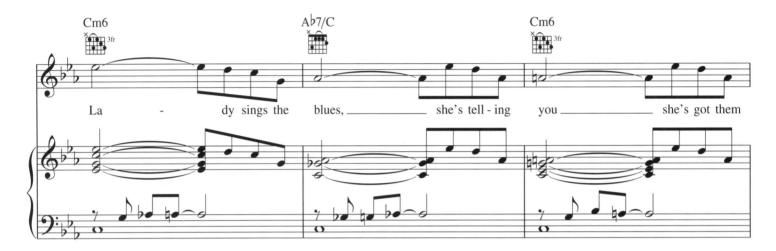

La - dy sings the blues, _____ she's tell - ing you _____ she's got them

bad. Now _____ the world will know, she's

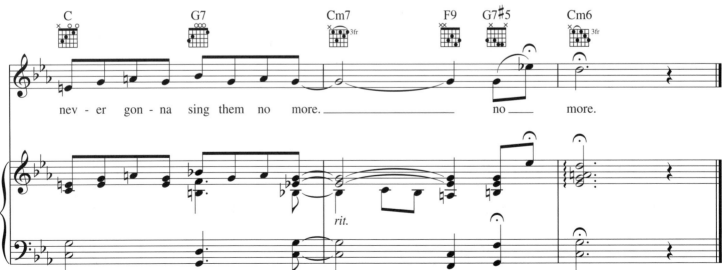

nev - er gon - na sing them no more. _____ no ___ more.

THE LAST TIME I SAW PARIS

from LADY, BE GOOD
from TILL THE CLOUDS ROLL BY

Lyrics by OSCAR HAMMERSTEIN II
Music by JEROME KERN

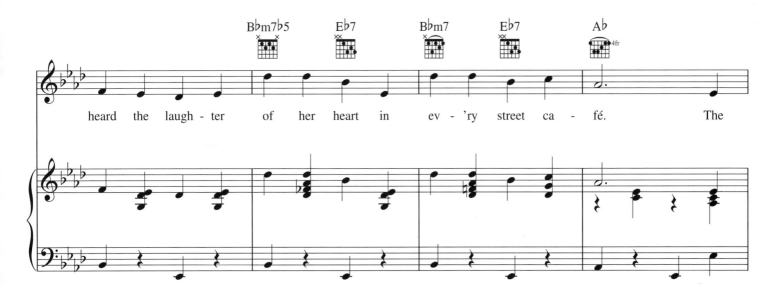

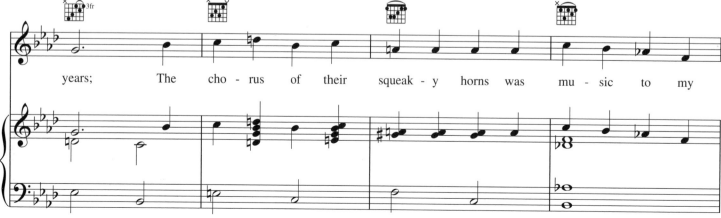

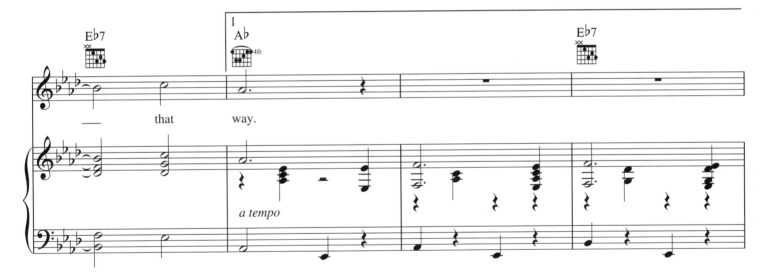

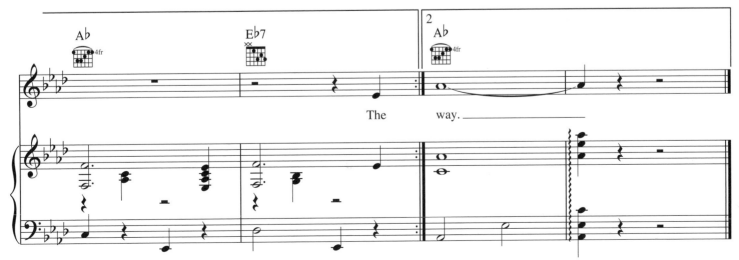

LONG AGO
(And Far Away)
from COVER GIRL

Words by IRA GERSHWIN
Music by JEROME KERN

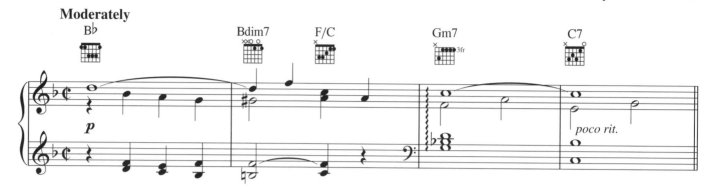

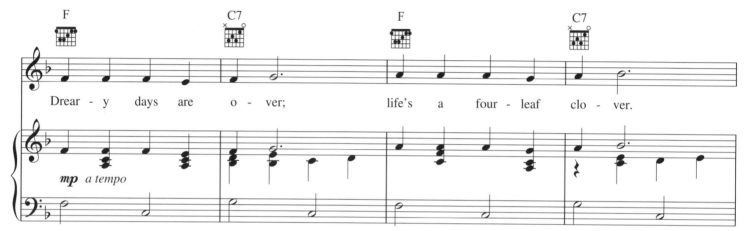

Drear - y days are o - ver; life's a four - leaf clo - ver.

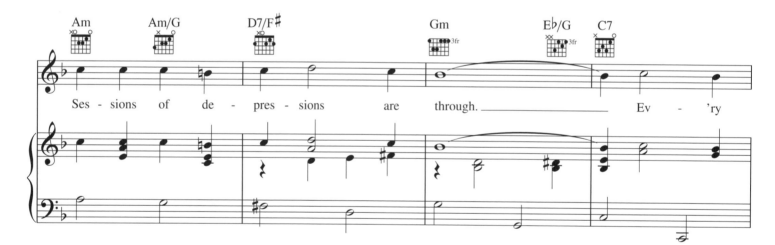

Ses - sions of de - pres - sions are through. _____ Ev - 'ry

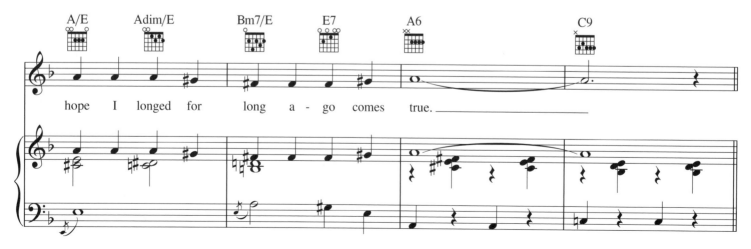

hope I longed for long a - go comes true. _____

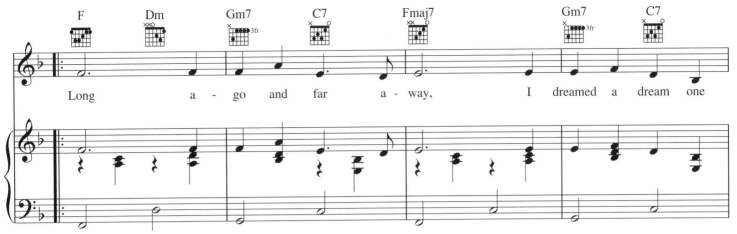

Long a - go and far a - way, I dreamed a dream one

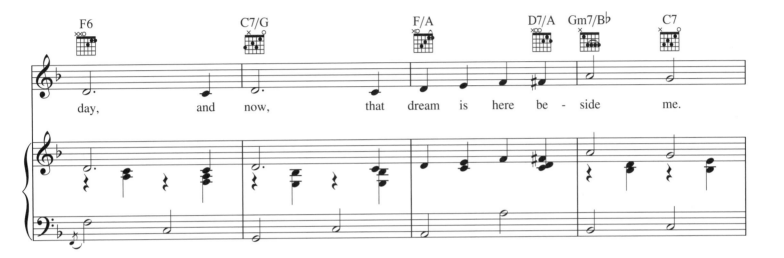

day, and now, that dream is here be - side me.

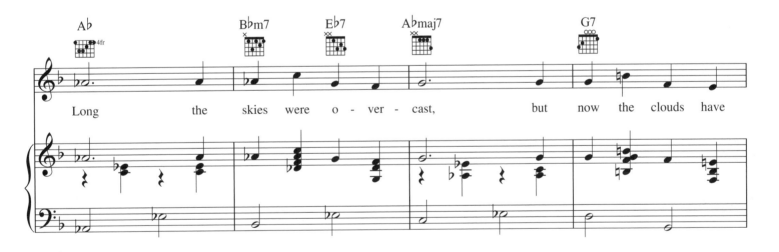

Long the skies were o - ver - cast, but now the clouds have

passed: You're here at last! _____ Chills run

up and down my spine, A-lad-din's lamp is mine, the dream I

dreamed was not de-nied me. Just one look and then I

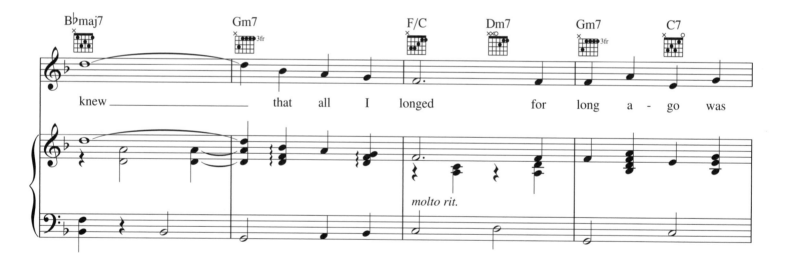

knew _____ that all I longed for long a-go was

molto rit.

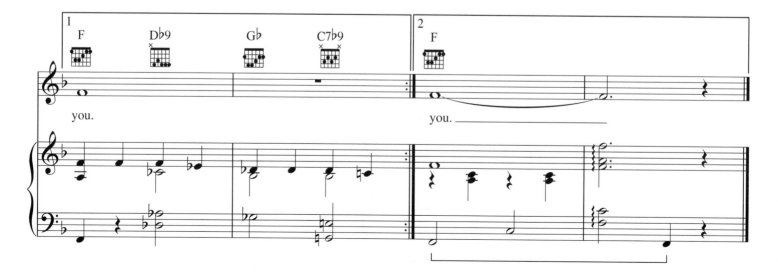

you.

you. _____

LOVE IS HERE TO STAY

from GOLDWYN FOLLIES
from AN AMERICAN IN PARIS

Music and Lyrics by GEORGE GERSHWIN
and IRA GERSHWIN

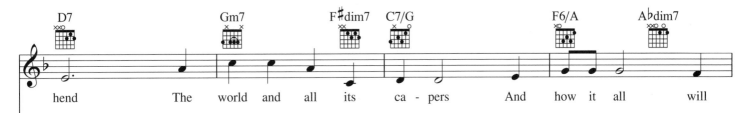

The more I read the pa-pers The less I com-pre-

hend The world and all its ca-pers And how it all will

end. Noth-ing seems to be last-ing, But

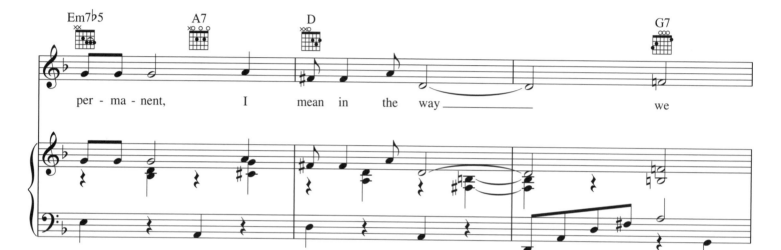

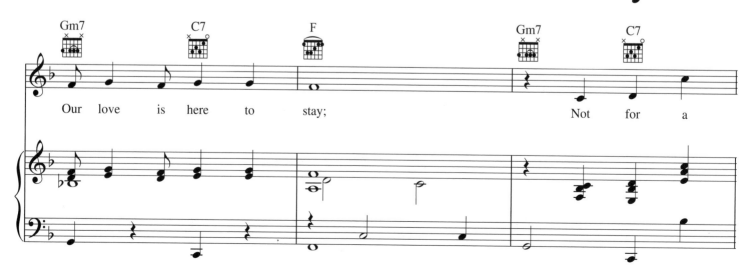

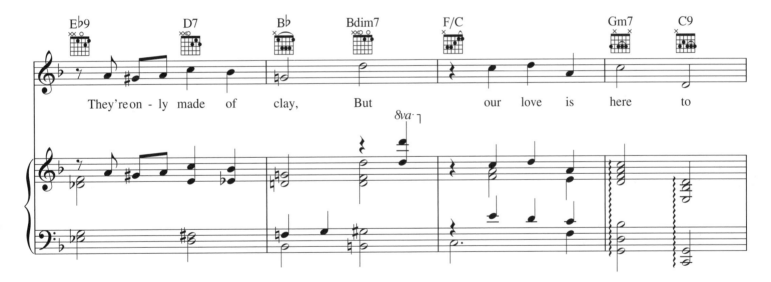

LULLABY OF BIRDLAND

Words by GEORGE DAVID WEISS
Music by GEORGE SHEARING

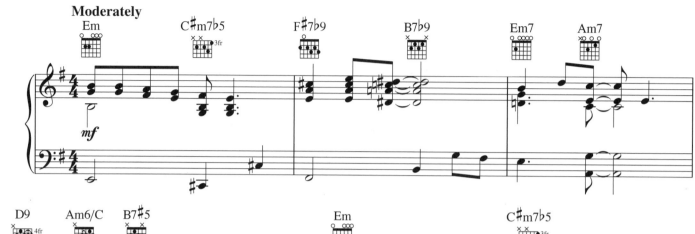

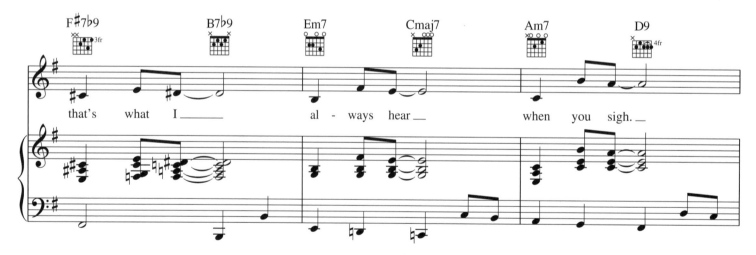

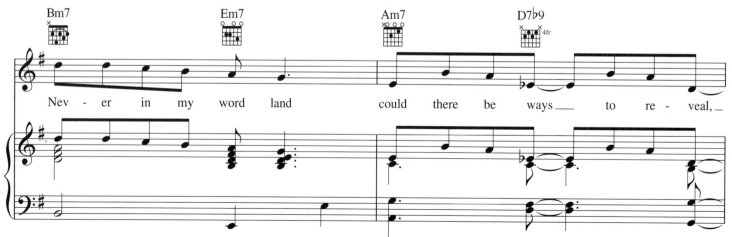

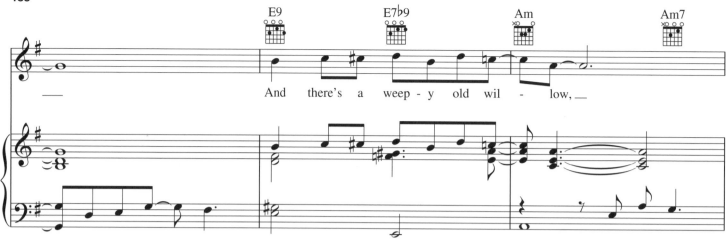

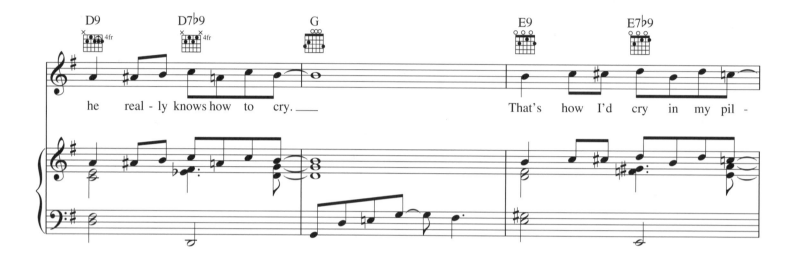

and we'll go _____ fly - in' high in Bird - land,

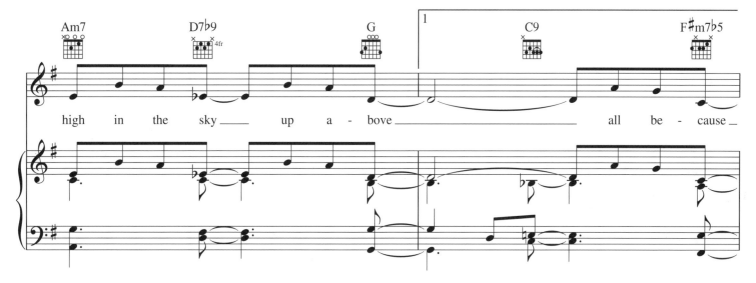

high in the sky _____ up a - bove _____ all be - cause _____

_____ we're in love. _____ all be - cause _____

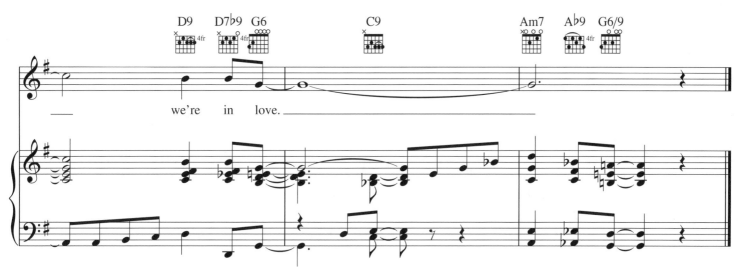

_____ we're in love. _____

MAIDEN VOYAGE

By HERBIE HANCOCK

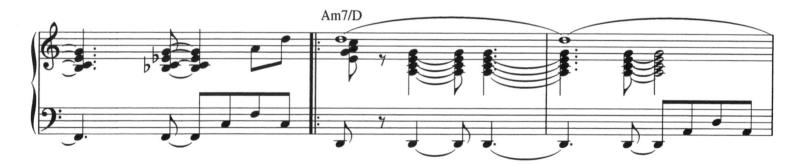

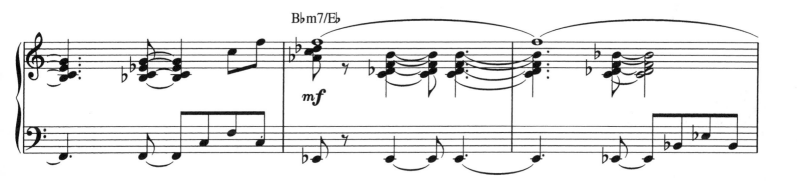

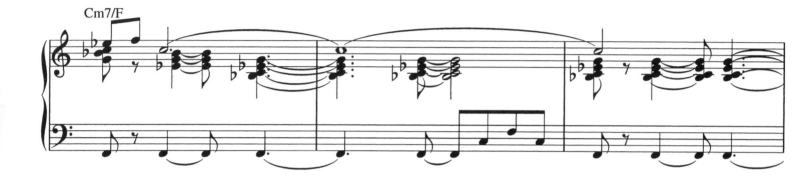

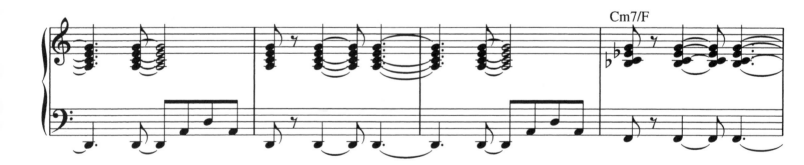

Repeat ad lib. and Fade

MEDITATION
(Meditacão)

Music by ANTONIO CARLOS JOBIM
Original Words by NEWTON MENDONÇA
English Words by NORMAN GIMBEL

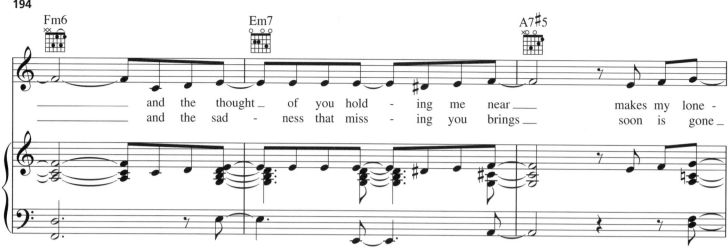

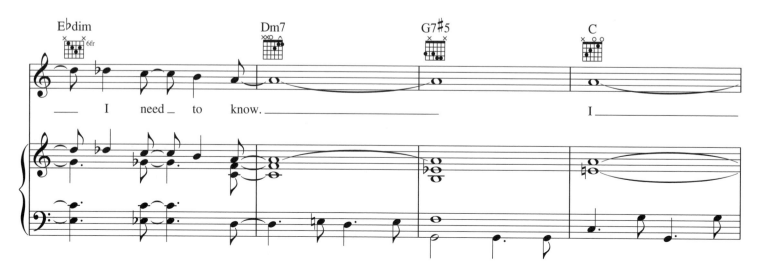

will wait for you 'til the sun

falls from out of the sky for what else can I do?

I will wait for you, med - i - tat -

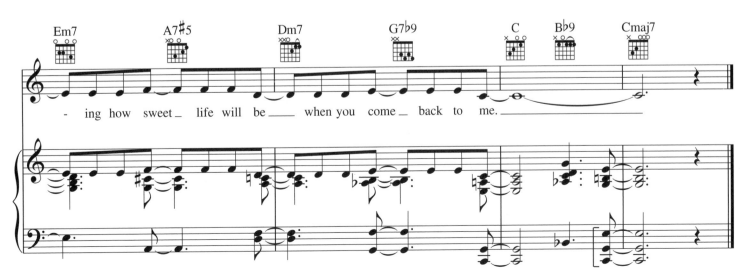

- ing how sweet life will be when you come back to me.

MAPLE LEAF RAG

Music by SCOTT JOPLIN

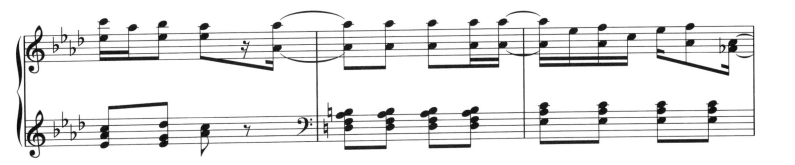

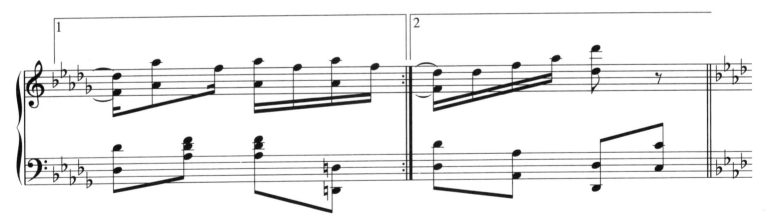

MY FAVORITE THINGS
from THE SOUND OF MUSIC

Lyrics by OSCAR HAMMERSTEIN II
Music by RICHARD RODGERS

Girls in white dress - es with blue sat - in sash - es, Snow-flakes that

stay on my nose and eye-lash - es, Sil - ver white win - ters that

melt in - to springs, These are a few of my fa - vor - ite things.

When the dog bites, When the bee stings,

MY FUNNY VALENTINE
from BABES IN ARMS

Words by LORENZ HART
Music by RICHARD RODGERS

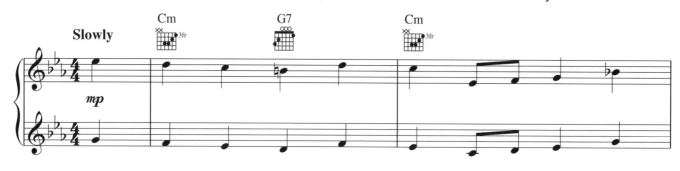

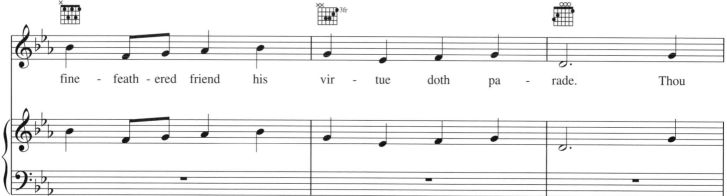

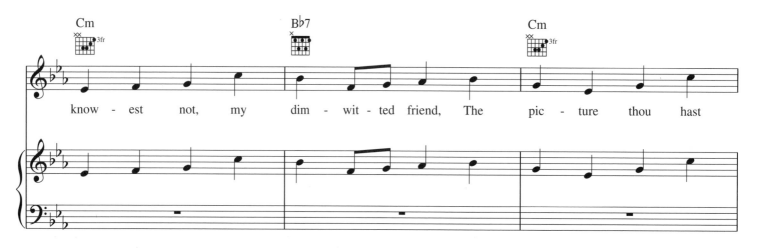

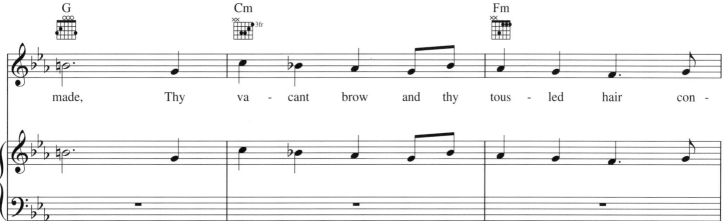

made, Thy va - cant brow and thy tous - led hair con -

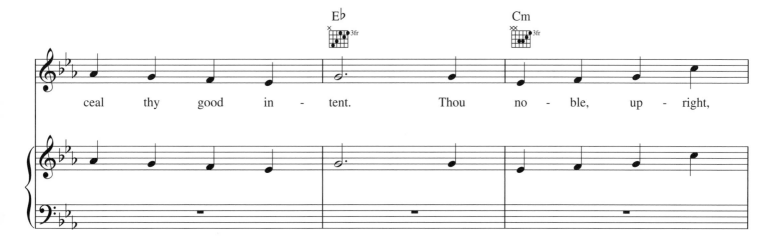

ceal thy good in - tent. Thou no - ble, up - right,

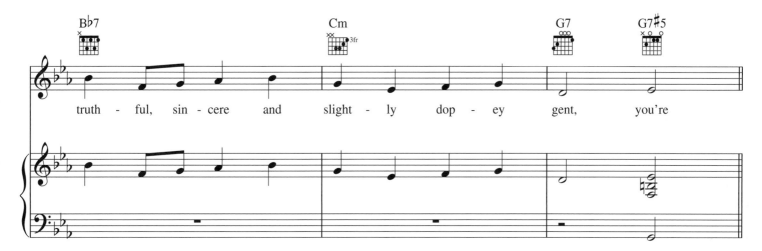

truth - ful, sin - cere and slight - ly dop - ey gent, you're

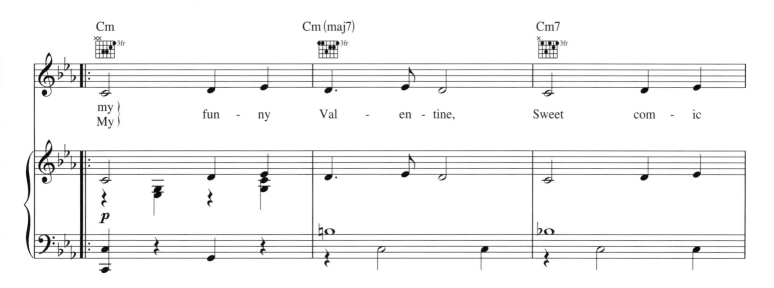

my } / My } fun - ny Val - en - tine, Sweet com - ic

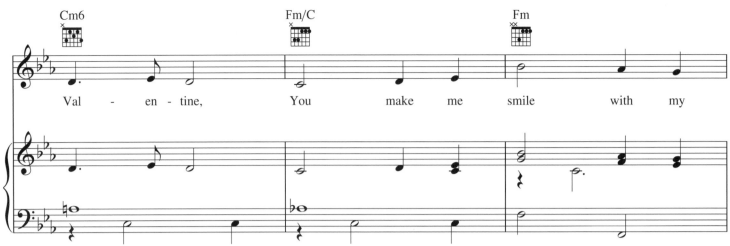

Val - en - tine, You make me smile with my

heart.

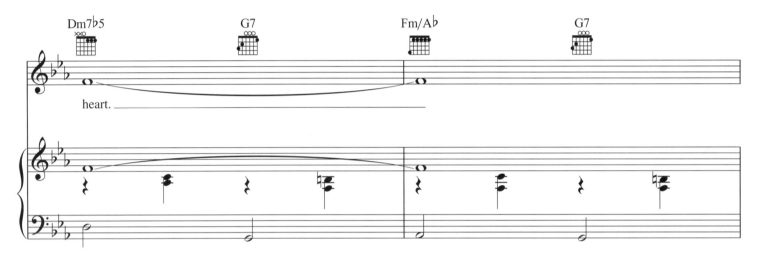

Your looks are laugh - a - ble, Un - pho - to -

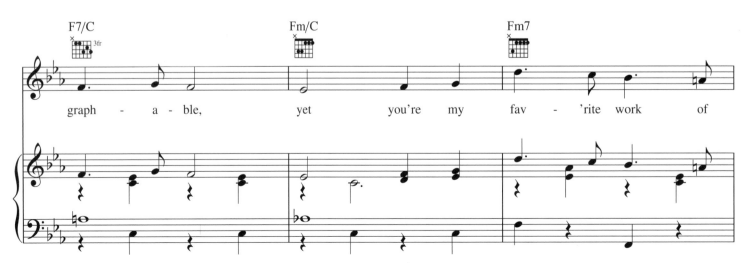

graph - a - ble, yet you're my fav - 'rite work of

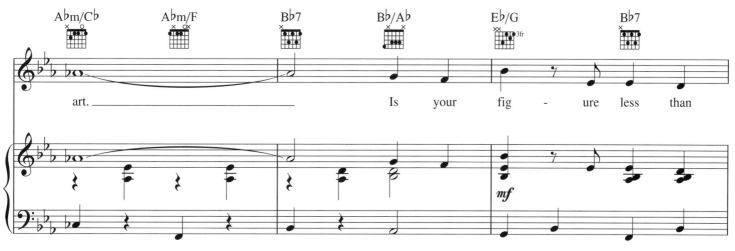

art. _____ Is your fig - ure less than

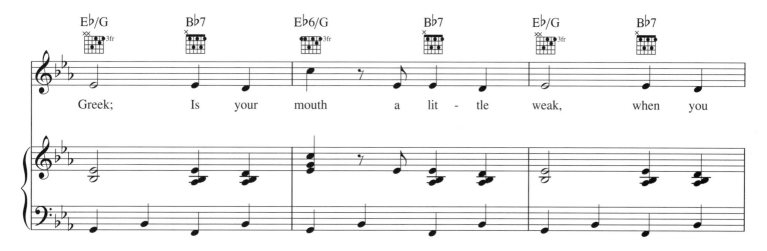

Greek; Is your mouth a lit - tle weak, when you

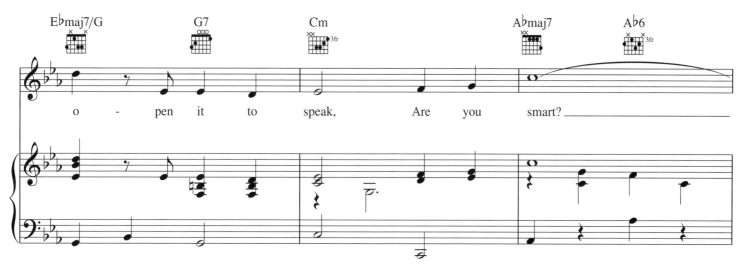

o - pen it to speak, Are you smart? _____

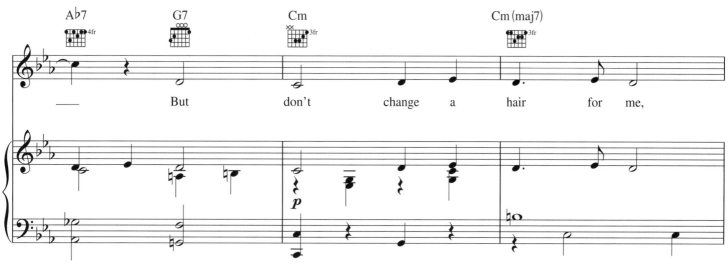

_____ But don't change a hair for me,

8vb

MY ONE AND ONLY LOVE

Words by ROBERT MELLIN
Music by GUY WOOD

Slowly

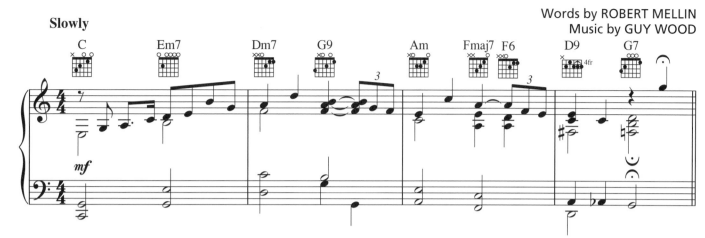

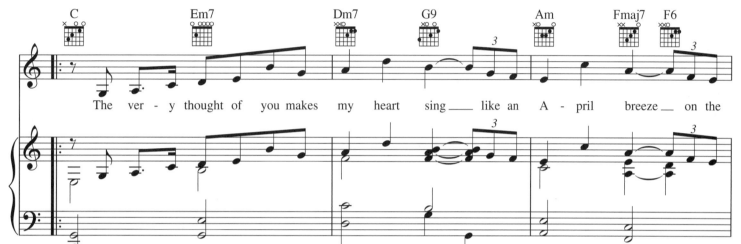

The ver - y thought of you makes my heart sing ___ like an A - pril breeze ___ on the

wings of spring, and you ap - pear in all your splen - dor, ___

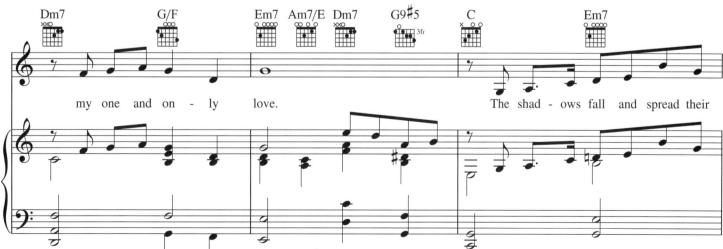

my one and on - ly love. The shad - ows fall and spread their

mys - tic charms ___ in the hush of night ___ while you're in my arms.

I feel your lips so warm and ten - der, _____ my one and on - ly

love. The touch ___ of your hand ___ is like heav - en, _____ a

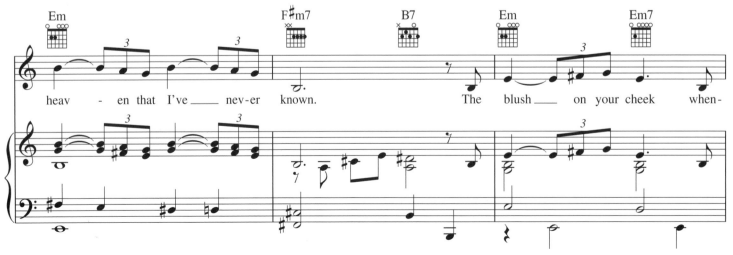

heav - en that I've ___ nev - er known. The blush ___ on your cheek when-

MY ROMANCE
from JUMBO

Words by LORENZ HART
Music by RICHARD RODGERS

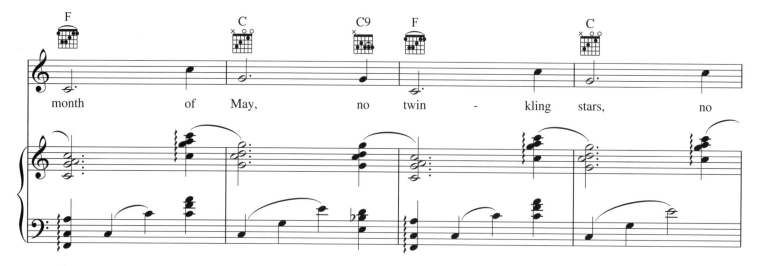

month of May, no twin - kling stars, no

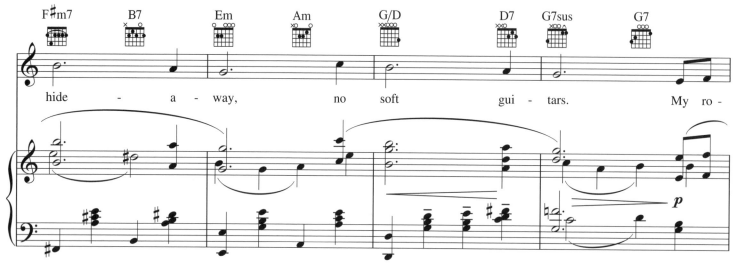

hide - a - way, no soft gui - tars. My ro -

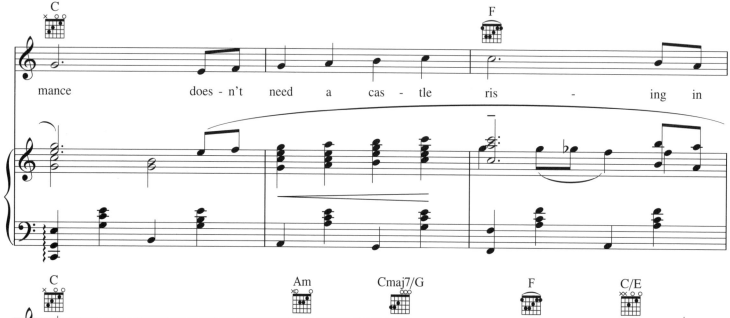

mance does - n't need a cas - tle ris - ing in

Spain, nor a dance to a con - stant - ly sur -

A NIGHT IN TUNISIA

By JOHN "DIZZY" GILLESPIE
and FRANK PAPARELLI

Moderately Fast

A NIGHTINGALE SANG IN BERKELEY SQUARE

Lyric by ERIC MASCHWITZ
Music by MANNING SHERWIN

When true lov-ers meet in May-fair, so the leg-ends tell, song birds sing, win-ter turns to spring, ev-'ry wind-ing street in May-fair falls be-neath the spell. I

*Pronounced "Bar-kley"

I may be right, I may be wrong, but I'm
This heart of mine beat loud and fast like a

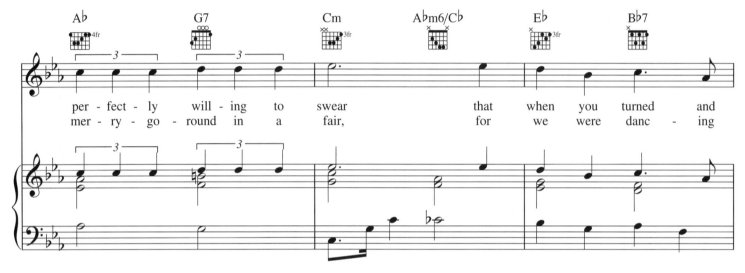

per - fect - ly will - ing to swear
mer - ry - go - round in a
that when you turned and
fair, for we were danc - ing

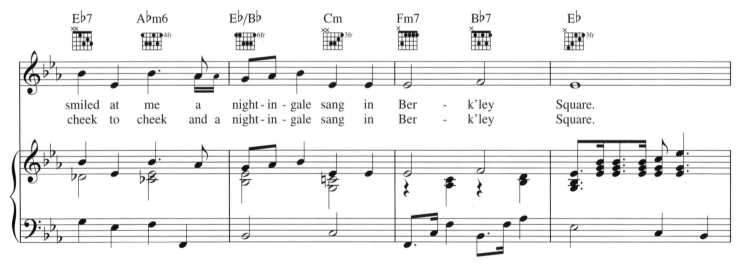

smiled at me a night - in - gale sang in Ber - k'ley Square.
cheek to cheek and a night - in - gale sang in Ber - k'ley Square.

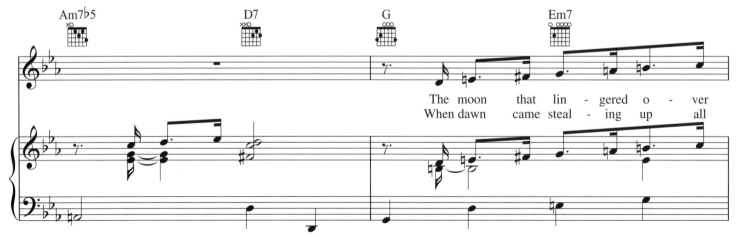

The moon that lin - gered o - ver
When dawn came steal - ing up all

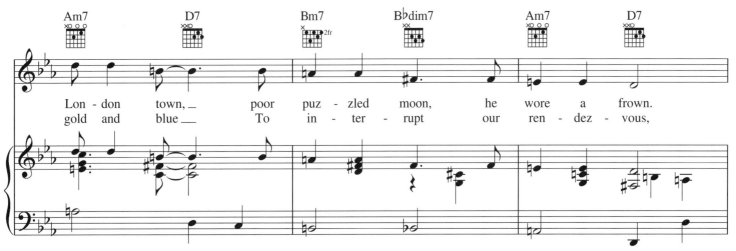

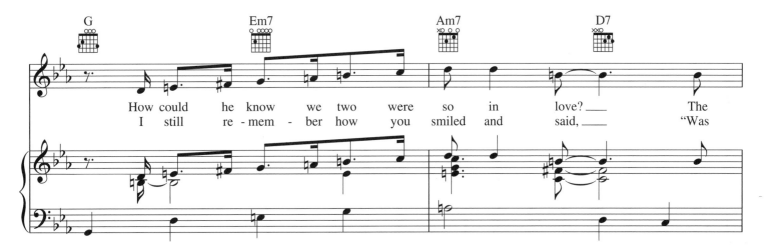

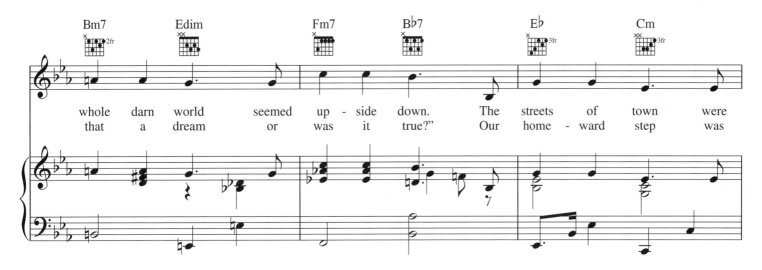

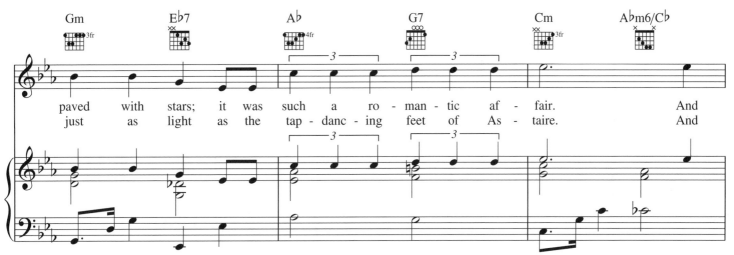

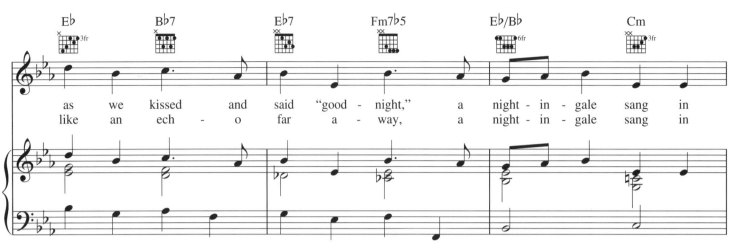

as we kissed and said "good - night," a night-in-gale sang in
like an ech - o far a - way, a night-in-gale sang in

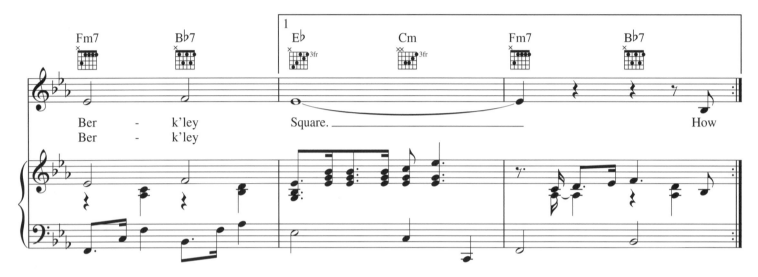

1

Ber - k'ley Square. _____ How
Ber - k'ley

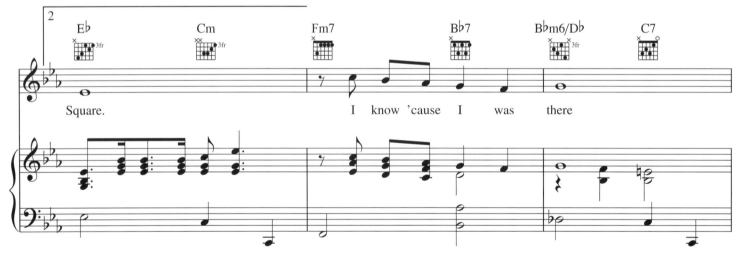

2

Square. I know 'cause I was there

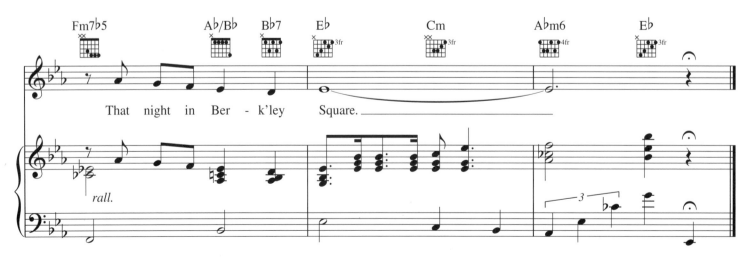

That night in Ber - k'ley Square. _____

rall.

PEOPLE WILL SAY WE'RE IN LOVE
from OKLAHOMA!

Lyrics by OSCAR HAMMERSTEIN II
Music by RICHARD RODGERS

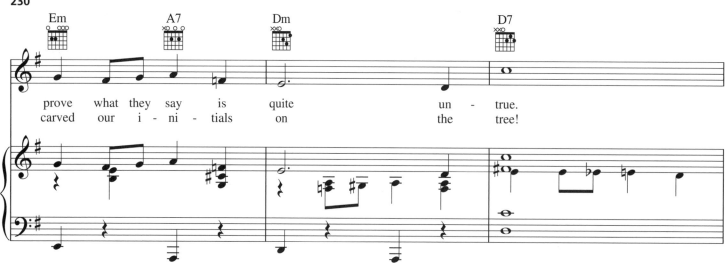

prove what they say is quite un - true.
carved our i - ni - tials on the tree!

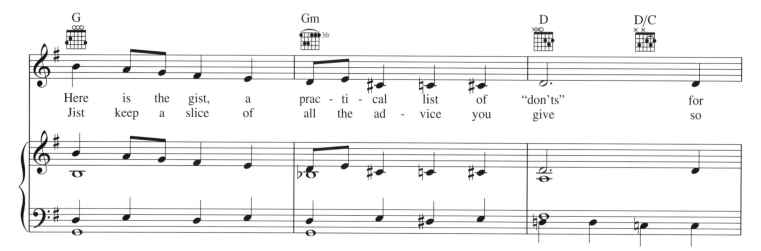

Here is the gist, a prac - ti - cal list of "don'ts" for
Jist keep a slice of all the ad - vice you give so

you. Don't throw _____ bou - quets at me.
free. Don't praise _____ my charm too much. _____

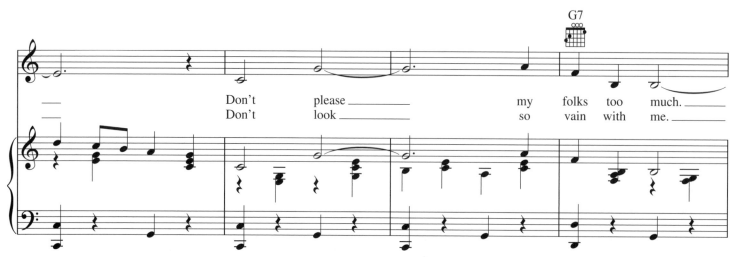

___ Don't please _____ my folks too much. _____
___ Don't look _____ so vain with me. _____

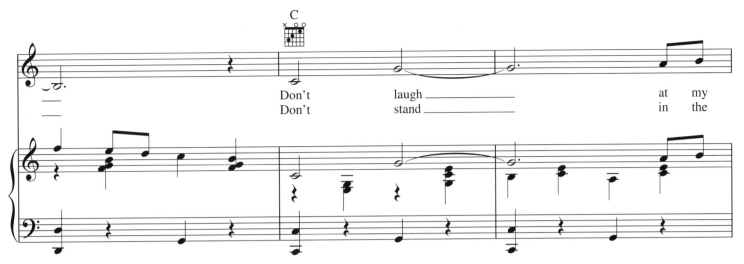

Don't laugh _____ at my
Don't stand _____ in the

jokes too much. _____ Peo - ple will say we're in
rain with me. _____ Peo - ple will say we're in

love! _____ Don't sigh _____ and
love! _____ Don't take _____ my

gaze at me. _____ Your sighs _____ are
arm too much. _____ Don't keep _____ your

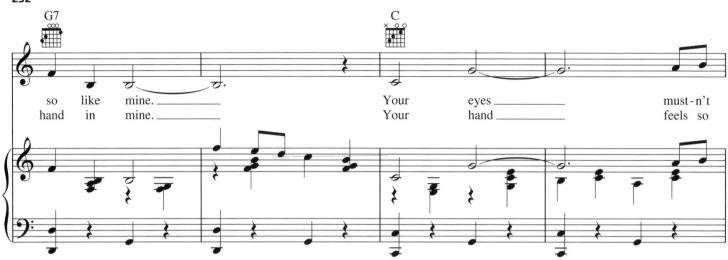

ONLY TRUST YOUR HEART

Words by SAMMY CAHN
Music by BENNY CARTER

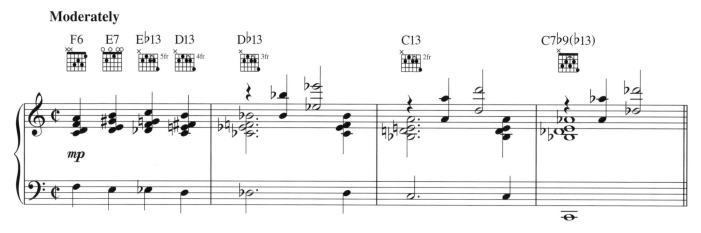

Moderately

Nev - er trust the stars _____ when you're a - bout to fall in

love. Look for hid - den signs _____ be - fore you

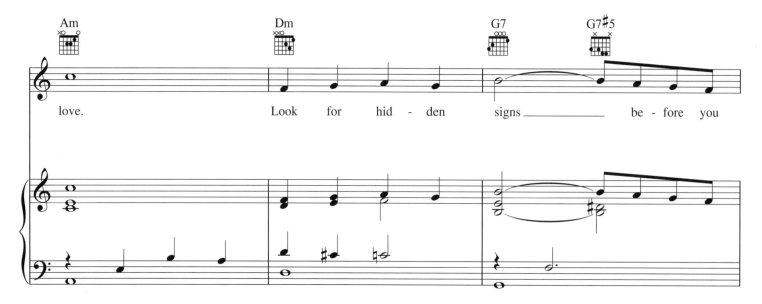

start to sigh. _____ Nev - er trust the

moon _____ when you're a - bout to taste his kiss.

He knows all the lines, _____ and he knows how to lie. _____

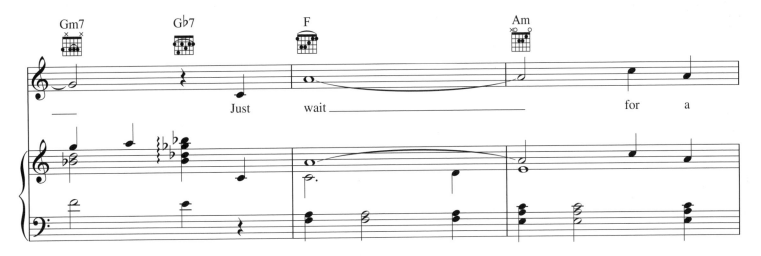

Just wait _____ for a

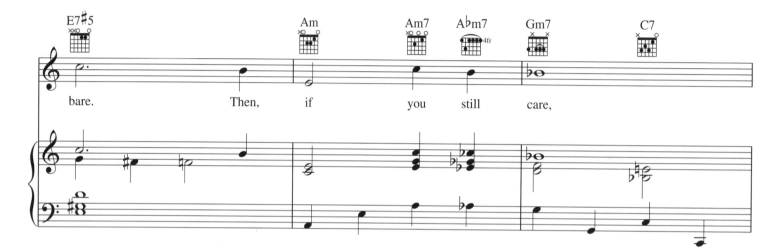

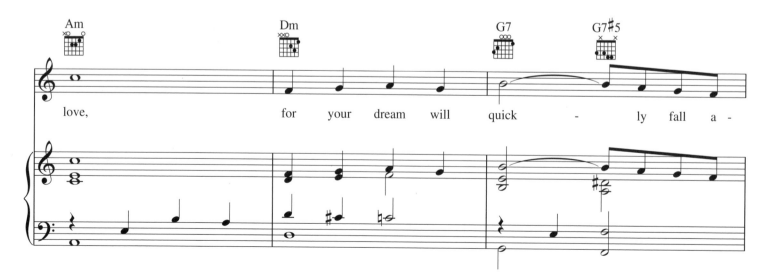

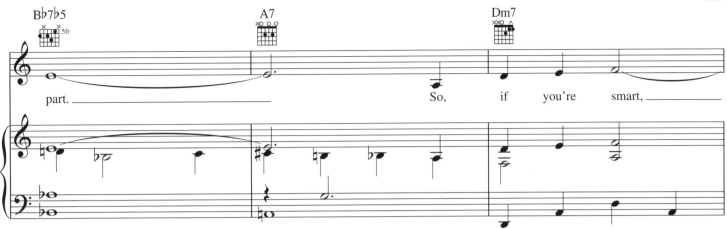

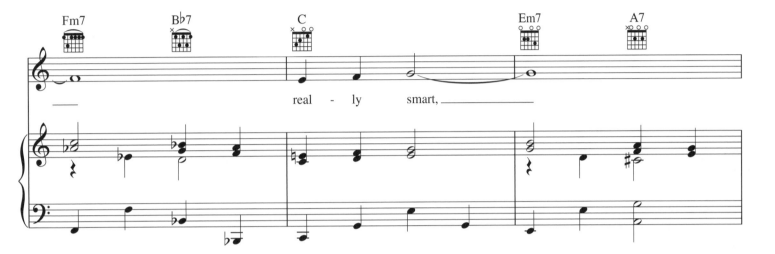

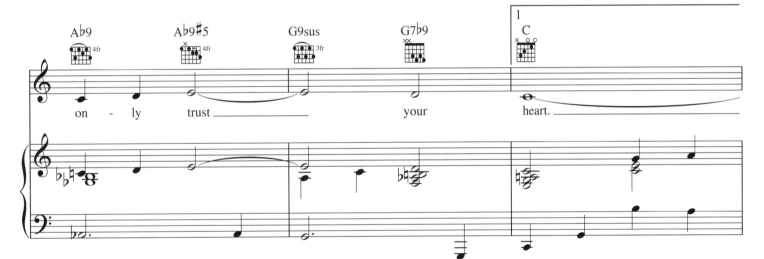

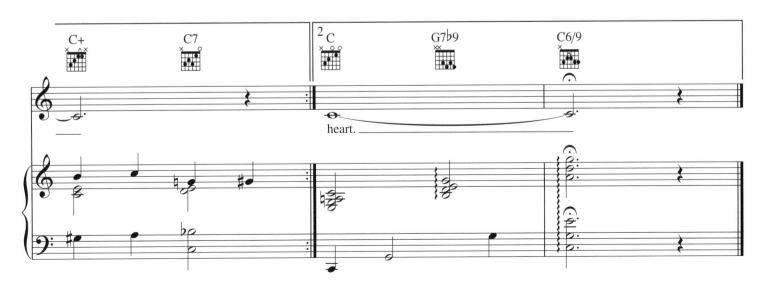

ORNITHOLOGY

By CHARLIE PARKER
and BENNIE HARRIS

Moderate jazz tempo

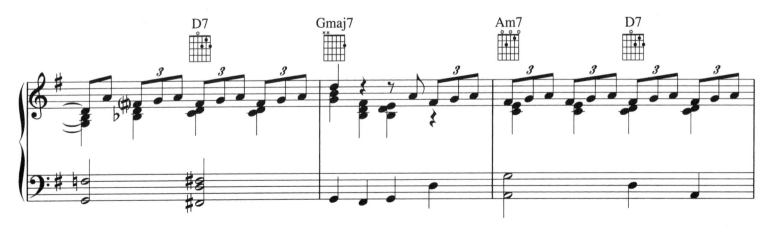

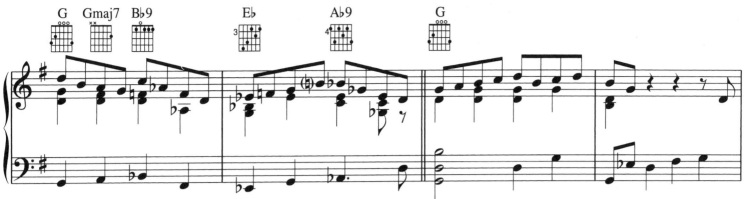

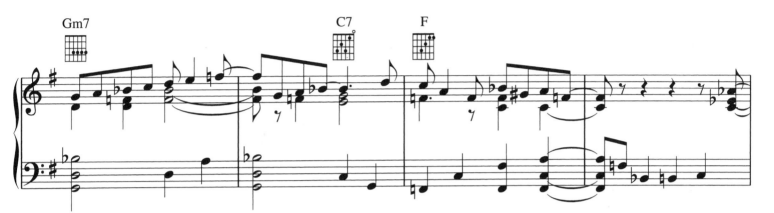

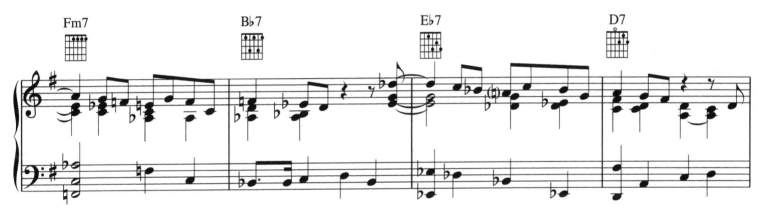

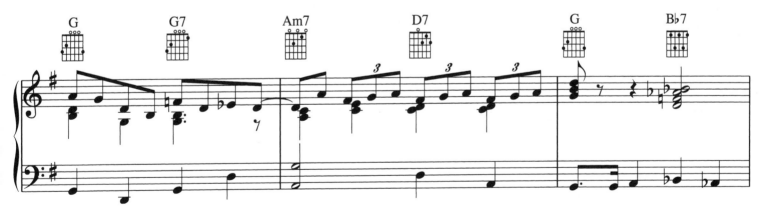

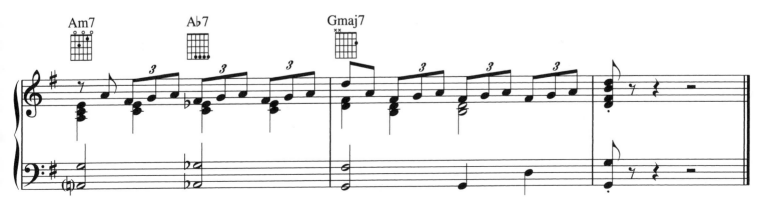

QUIET NIGHTS OF QUIET STARS
(Corcovado)

English Words by GENE LEES
Original Words & Music by ANTONIO CARLOS JOBIM

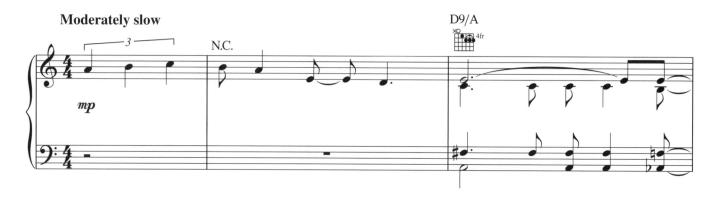

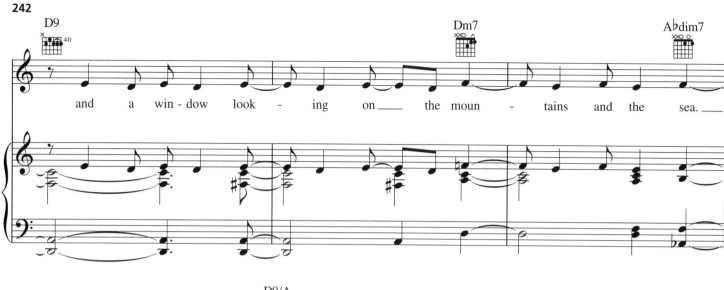

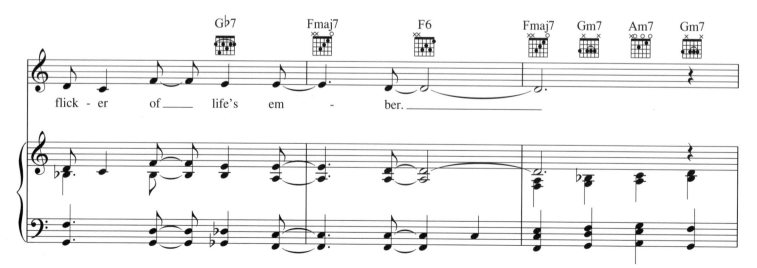

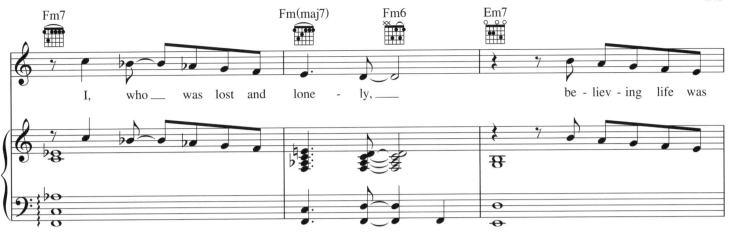

I, who __ was lost and lone - ly, __ be - liev - ing life was

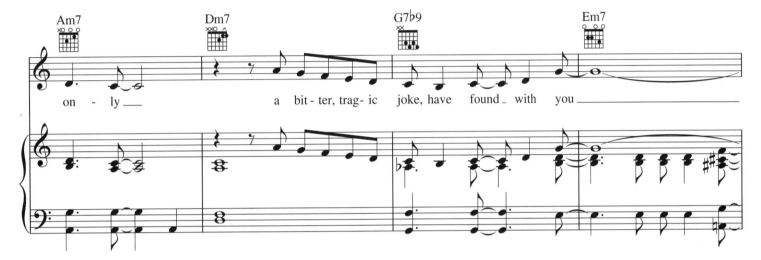

on - ly __ a bit - ter, trag - ic joke, have found __ with you __

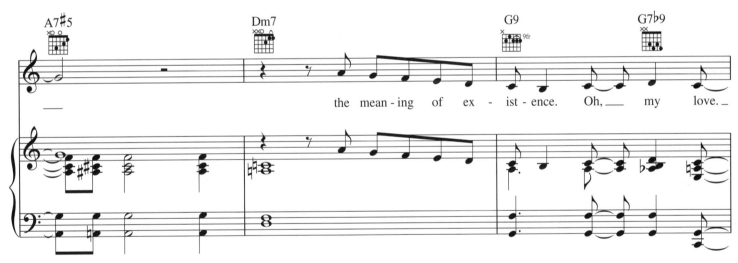

the mean - ing of ex - ist - ence. Oh, __ my love. __

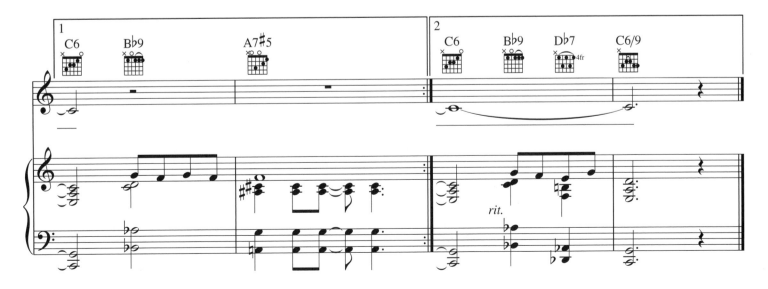

rit.

'ROUND MIDNIGHT

Words by BERNIE HANIGHEN
Music by THELONIOUS MONK
and COOTIE WILLIAMS

Moderately slow, in 2

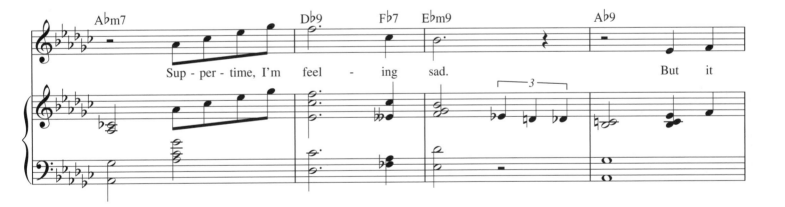

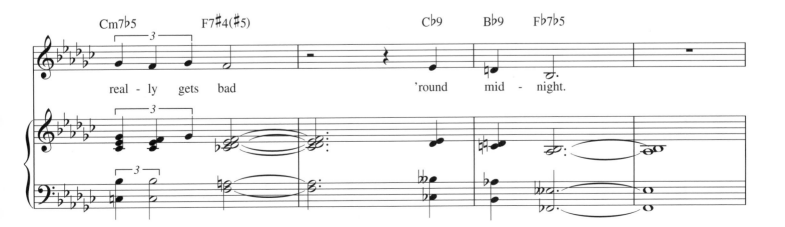

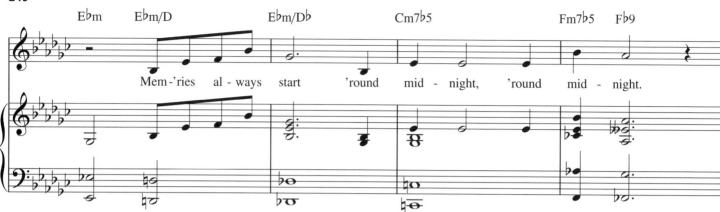

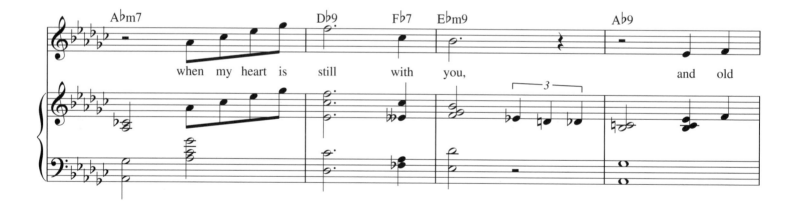

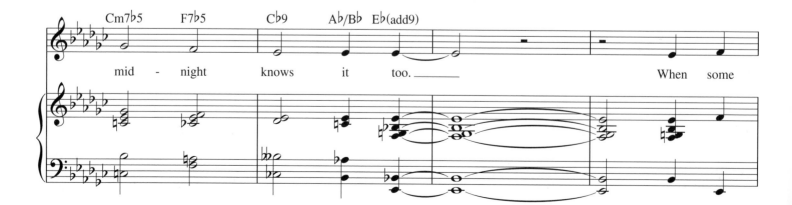

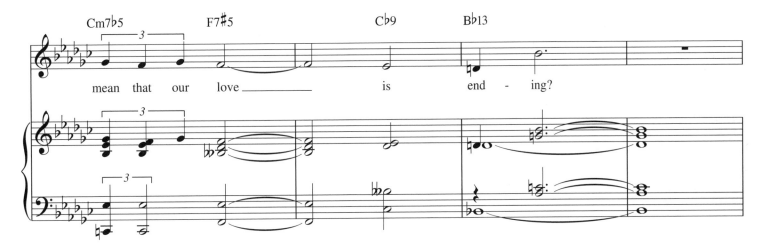

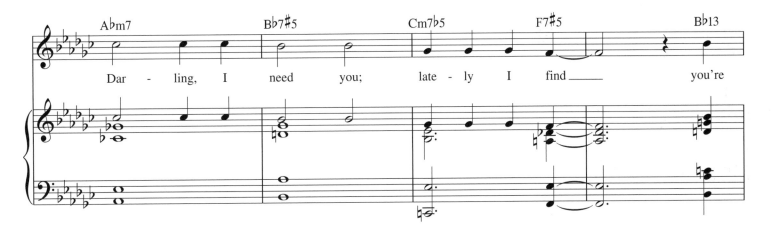

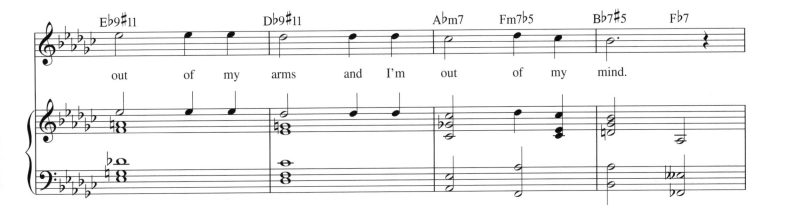

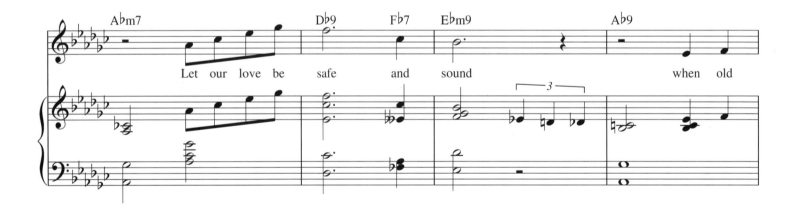

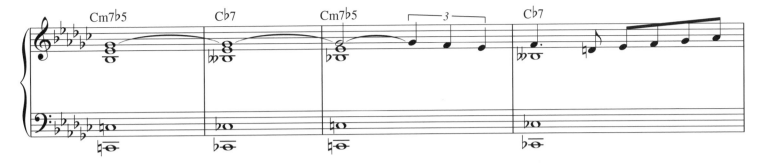

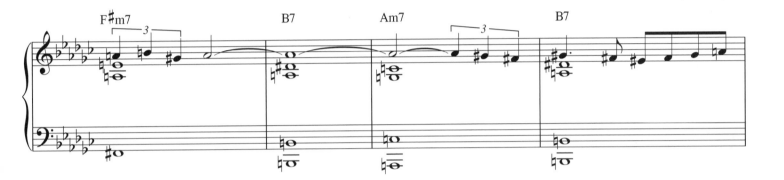

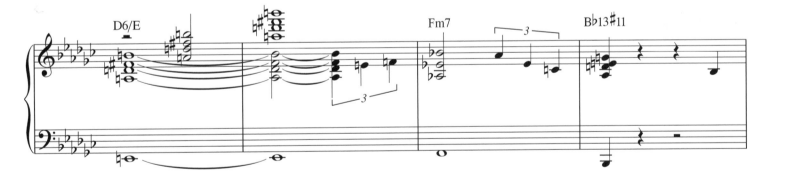

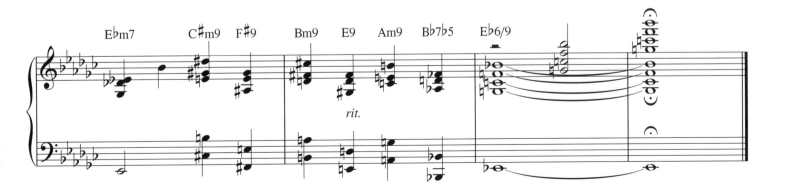

ROUTE 66

By BOBBY TROUP

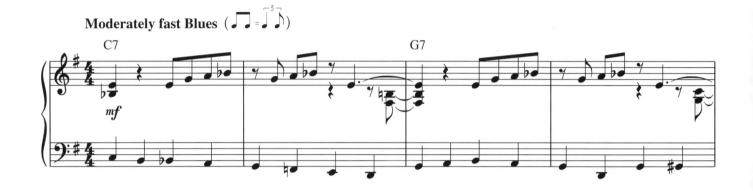

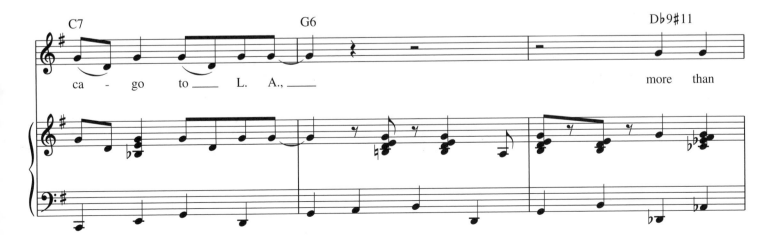

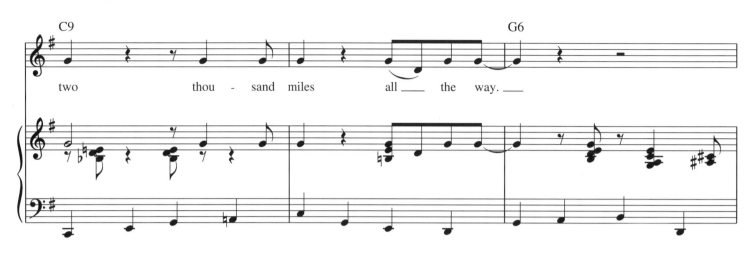

two thou - sand miles all ___ the way. ___

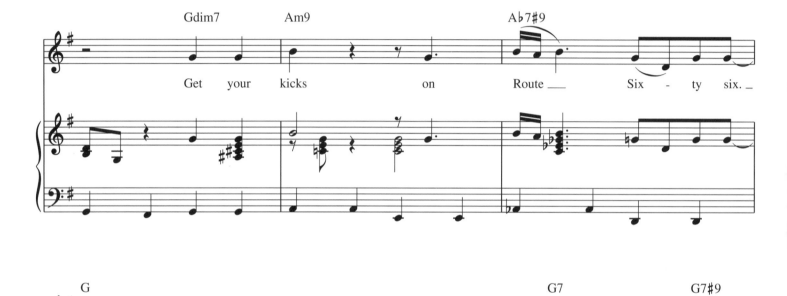

Get your kicks on Route ___ Six - ty six. ___

___ Now you go ___ through Saint Lou - ie,

Jop - lin Mis - sou - ri, and O - kla - ho - ma Cit - y looks might - y pret - ty. You'll

see ___ Am - a - ril - lo, Gal - lup, New

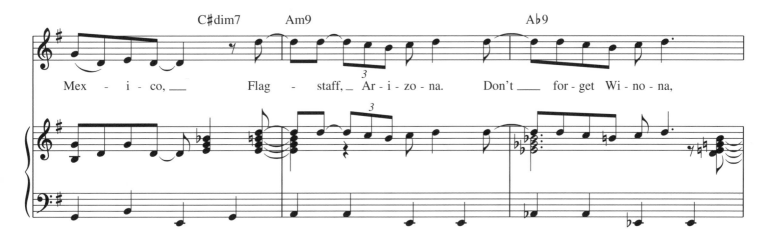

Mex - i - co, ___ Flag - staff, _ Ar - i - zo - na. Don't ___ for - get Wi - no - na,

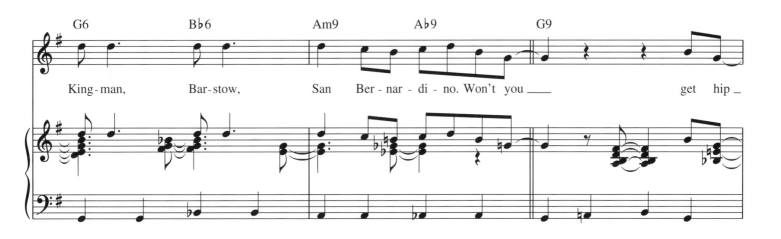

King - man, Bar - stow, San Ber - nar - di - no. Won't you ___ get hip _

_ to this time - ly tip, ___ when _ you make _

that Cal - i - for - nia trip. ___

Get ___ your kicks ___ on Route ___ Six - ty six. ___

Get your kicks ___ on

Route ___ Six - ty six. ___

SAMBA DE ORFEU

Words by ANTONIO MARIA
Music by LUIZ BONFA

Que-ro vi - ver, ___ que - ro sam - bar ___

A - té ___ sen - tir ___ a es - sên-cia da vi - da, Me ___ fal - ta - ar. ___

___ Que-ro ___ sam - bar, ___ que - ro vi - ver. ___

SATIN DOLL
from SOPHISTICATED LADIES

Words by JOHNNY MERCER and BILLY STRAYHORN
Music by DUKE ELLINGTON

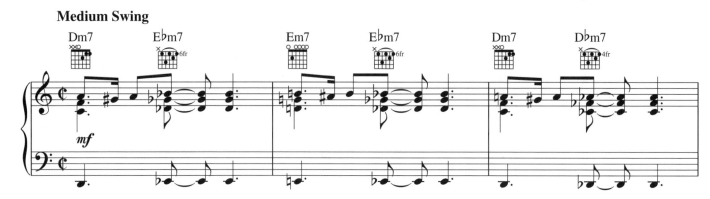

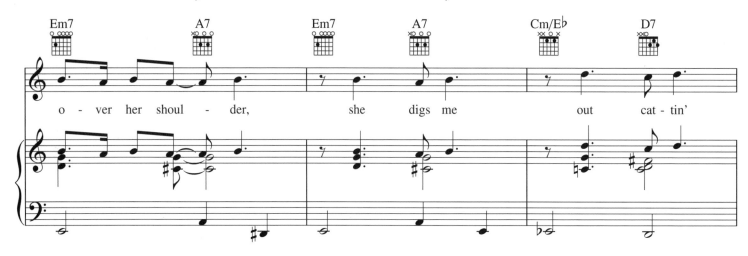

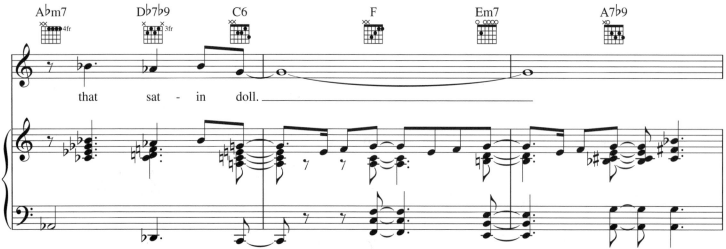

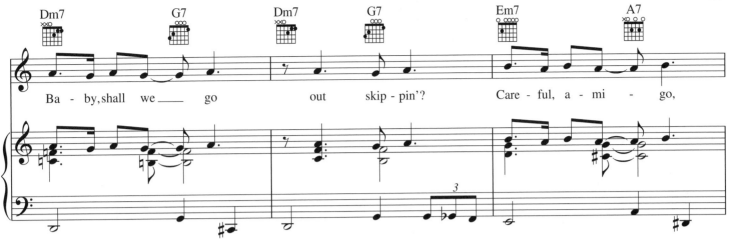

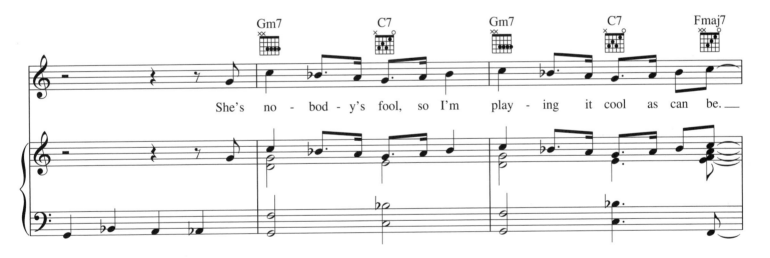

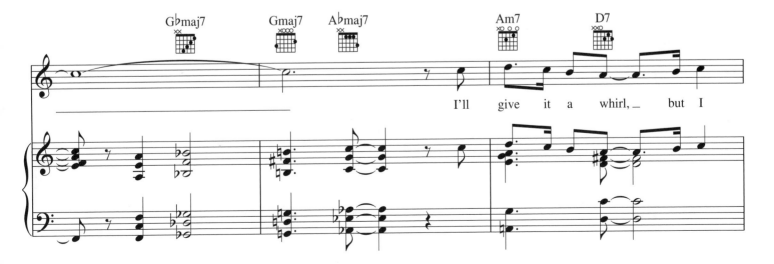

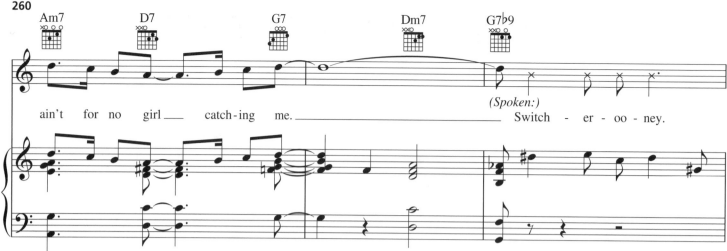

ain't for no girl___ catch-ing me._____ *(Spoken:)* Switch - er - oo - ney.

Tel - e-phone num - bers well you know, do - ing my rhum - bas

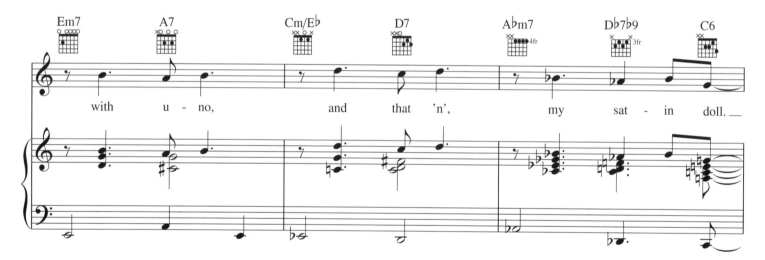

with u - no, and that 'n', my sat - in doll.___

SONG FOR MY FATHER

By HORACE SILVER

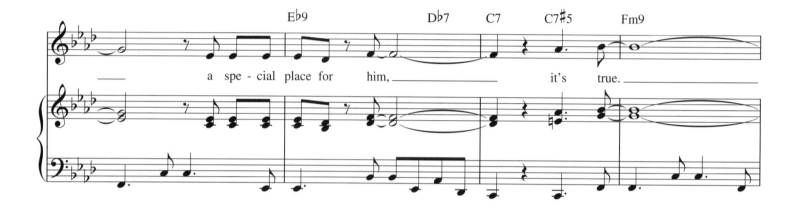

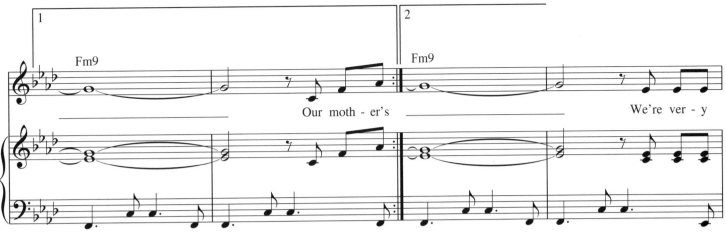

Our moth-er's We're ver-y

proud to be in his bi-og-ra-phy.

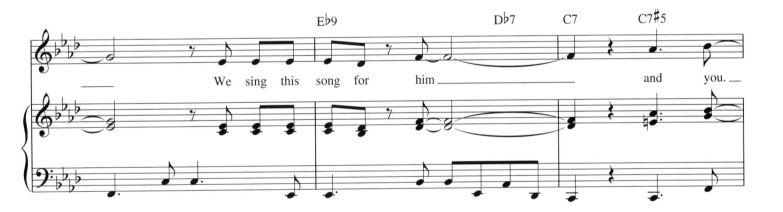

We sing this song for him and you.

SKYLARK

Words by JOHNNY MERCER
Music by HOAGY CARMICHAEL

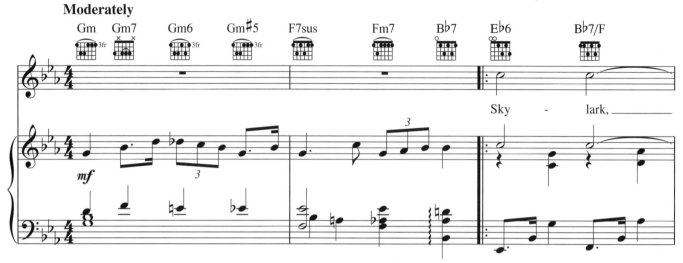

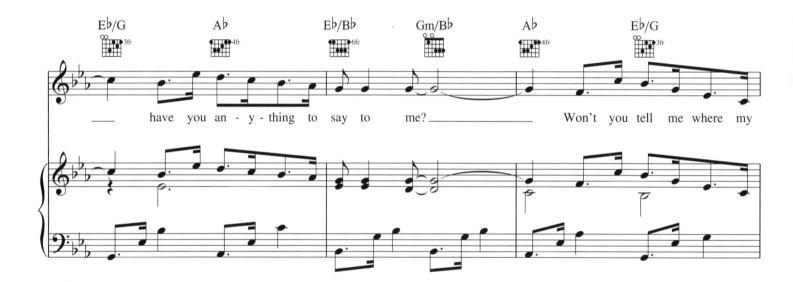

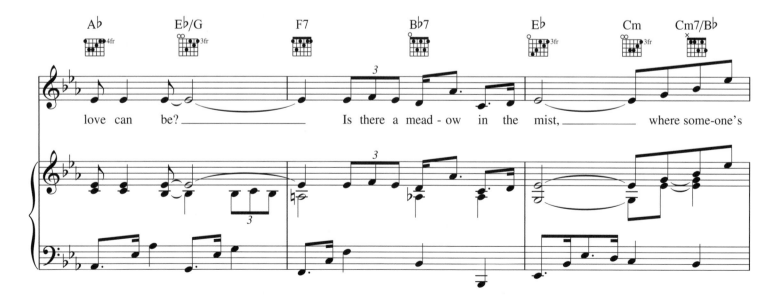

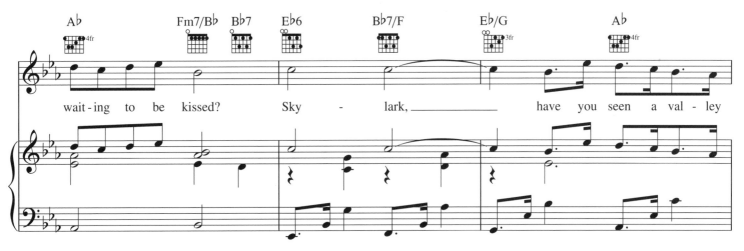

wait-ing to be kissed? Sky - lark, _____ have you seen a val - ley

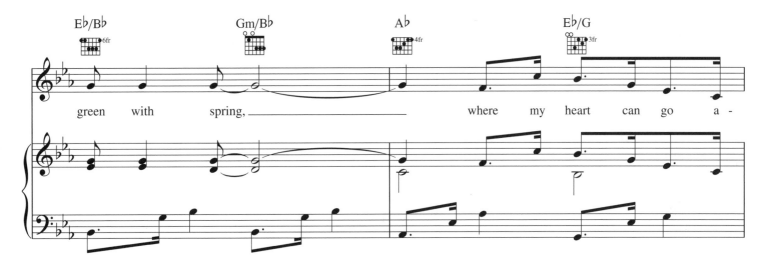

green with spring, _____ where my heart can go a -

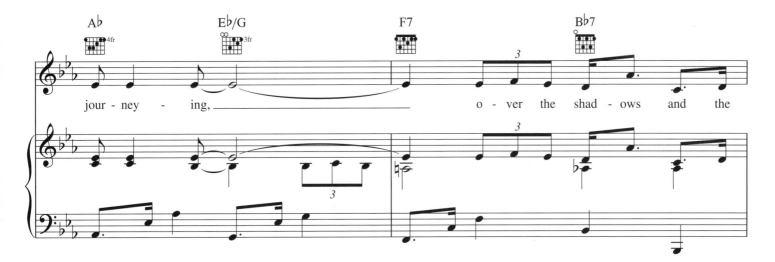

jour - ney - ing, _____ o - ver the shad - ows and the

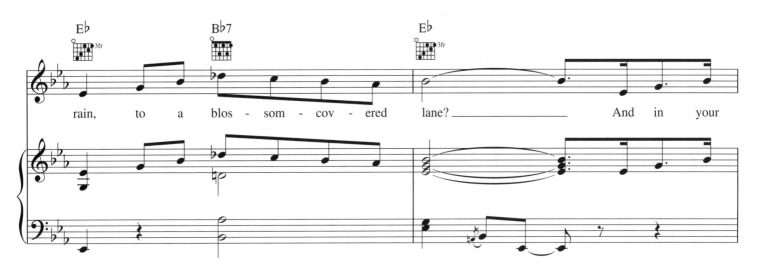

rain, to a blos - som - cov - ered lane? _____ And in your

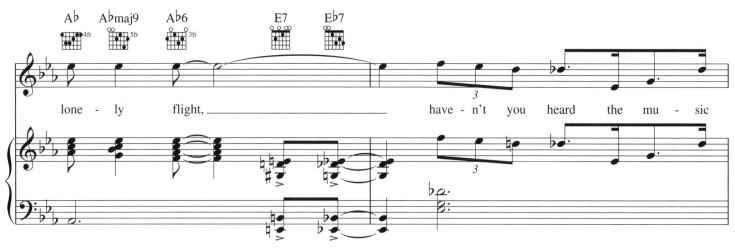

lone - ly flight, _____ have - n't you heard the mu - sic

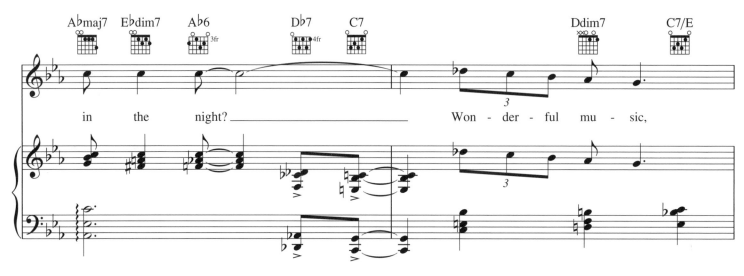

in the night? _____ Won - der - ful mu - sic,

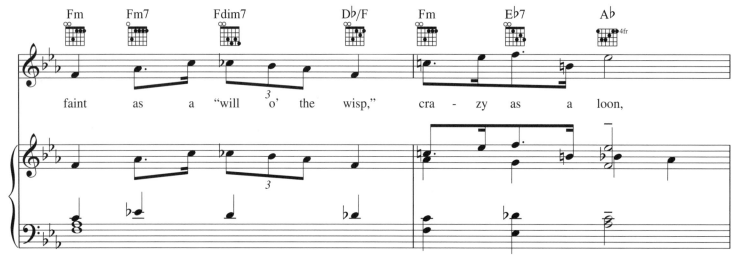

faint as a "will o' the wisp," cra - zy as a loon,

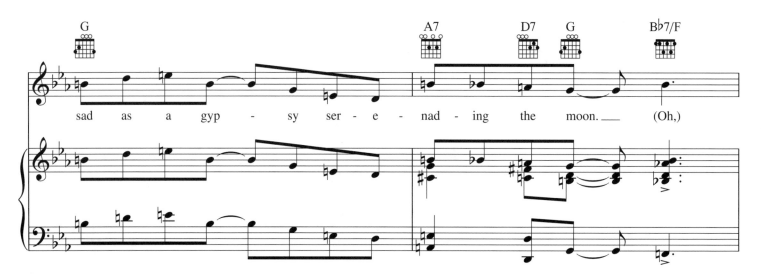

sad as a gyp - sy ser - e - nad - ing the moon. ___ (Oh,)

Sky - lark, _____ I don't know if you can

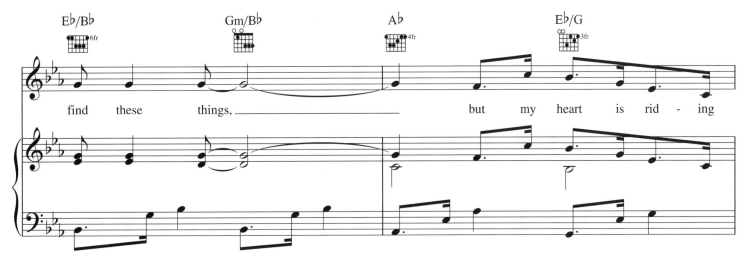

find these things, _____ but my heart is rid - ing

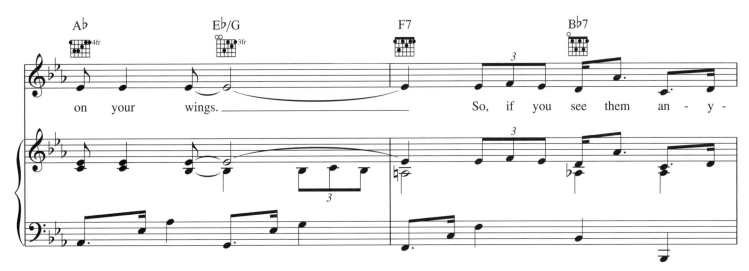

on your wings. _____ So, if you see them an - y -

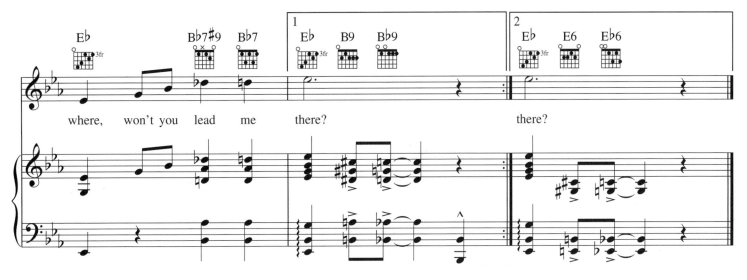

where, won't you lead me there? there?

THE SONG IS YOU

from MUSIC IN THE AIR

Lyrics by OSCAR HAMMERSTEIN II
Music by JEROME KERN

(I Can Recall)
SPAIN

Lyrics by ARTIE MAREN and AL JARREAU
Music by CHICK COREA and JOAQUIN RODRIGO
Introduction after a theme in the 2nd Movement
of the Concerto D'Aranjuez by JOAQUIN RODRIGO

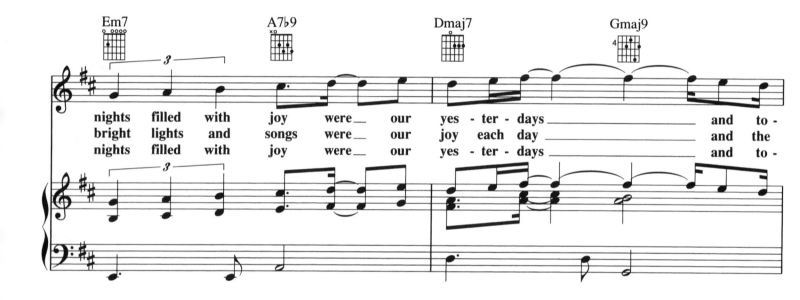

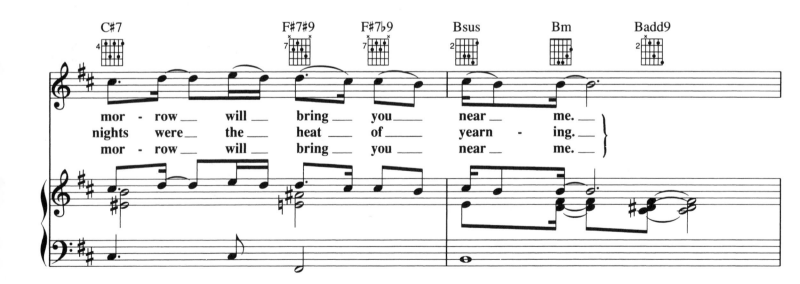

TAKE THE "A" TRAIN

Words and Music by
BILLY STRAYHORN

Moderately fast Swing

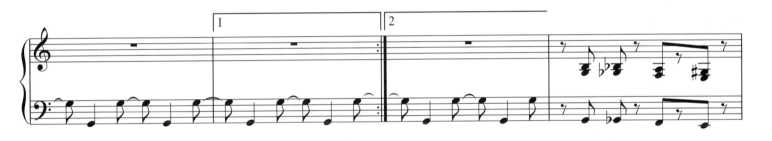

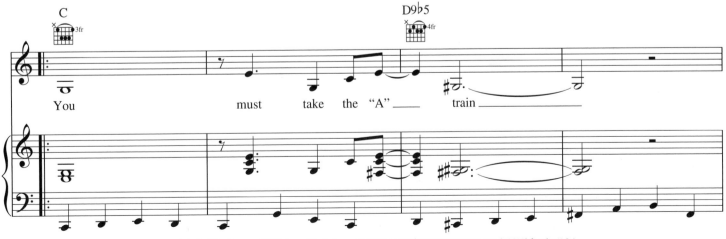

You must take the "A" ____ train ____

to go to Sug - ar Hill way up in Har - lem.

If you miss the "A" train,

you'll find you've missed the quick - est way to

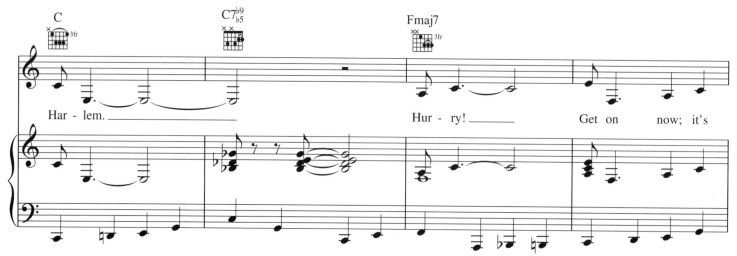

Har - lem. Hur - ry! Get on now; it's

com - ing! _____ Lis - ten _____ to those rails a -

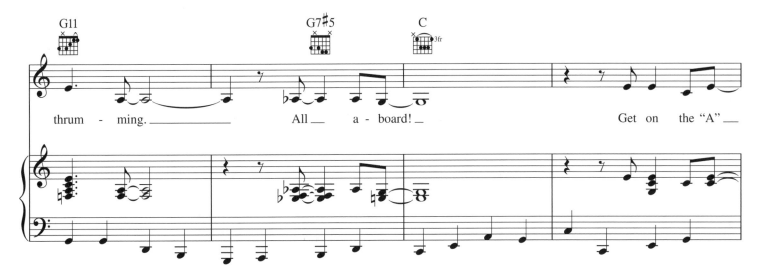

thrum - ming. _____ All __ a - board! __ Get on the "A" __

_____ train. _____ Soon you will be on Sug - ar Hill in

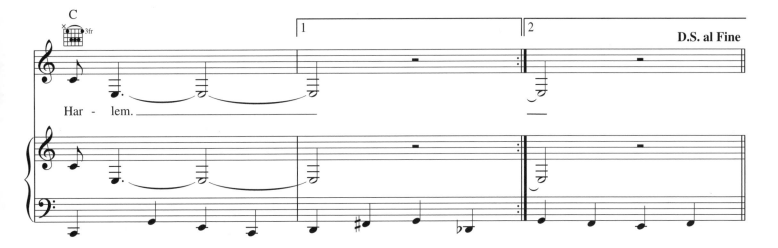

Har - lem. _____

D.S. al Fine

TENDERLY
from TORCH SONG

Lyric by JACK LAWRENCE
Music by WALTER GROSS

Moderately

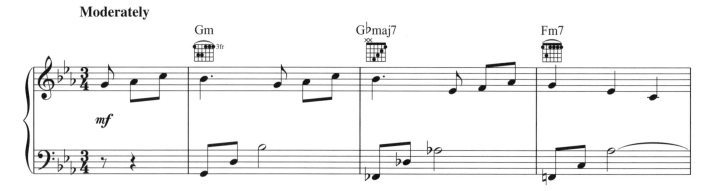

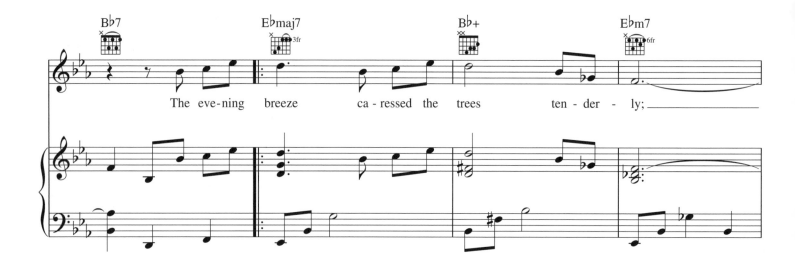

The eve-ning breeze ca-ressed the trees ten - der - ly; ___

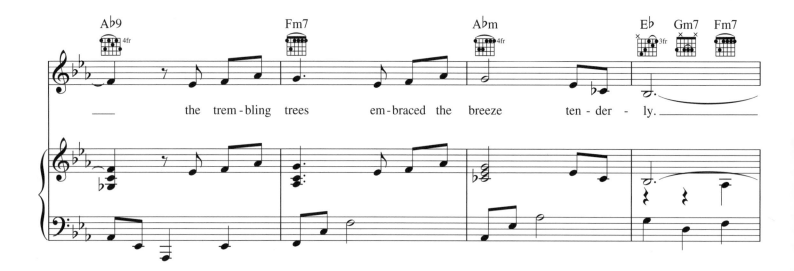

___ the trem-bling trees em-braced the breeze ten - der - ly. ___

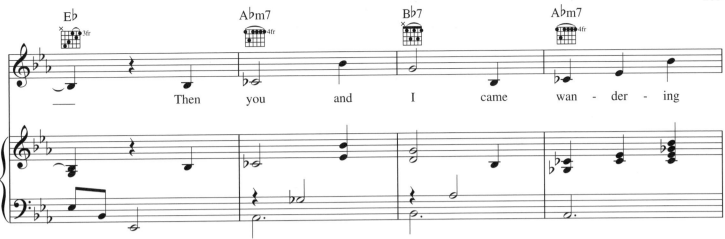

Then you and I came wan - der - ing

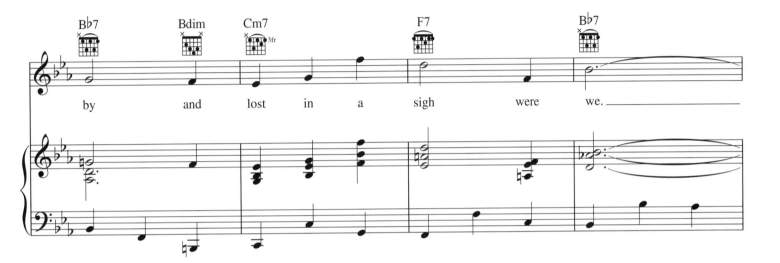

by and lost in a sigh were we. ___

___ The shore was kissed by sea and mist ten - der - ly. ___

___ I can't for - get how two hearts met breath - less -

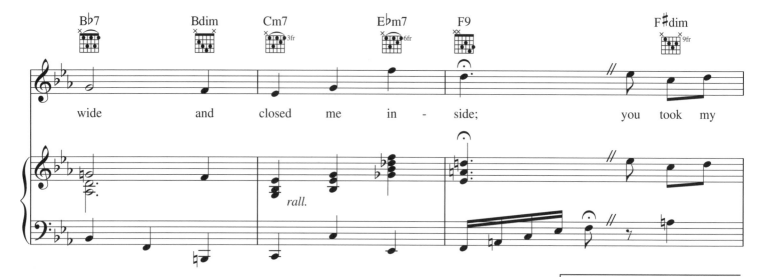

THERE WILL NEVER BE ANOTHER YOU

from the Motion Picture ICELAND

Lyric by MACK GORDON
Music by HARRY WARREN

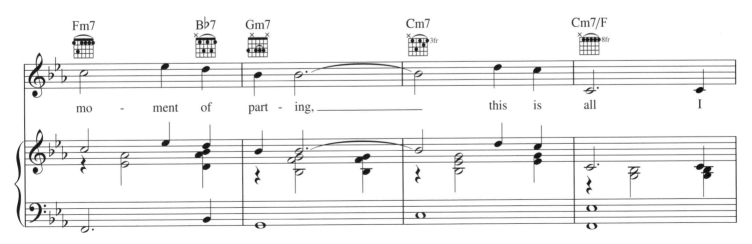

This is our last dance to-geth-er, to-

night soon will be long a-go. And in our

mo-ment of part-ing, this is all I

want you to know: _____ There will be man-y

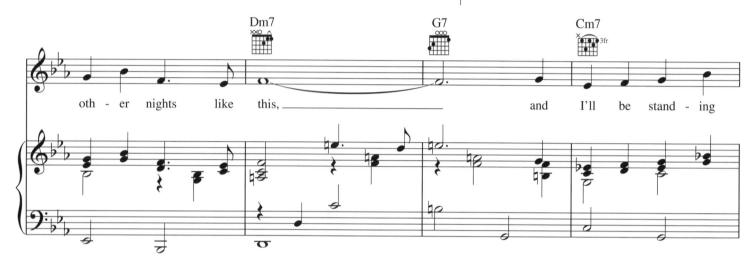

oth - er nights like this, _____ and I'll be stand - ing

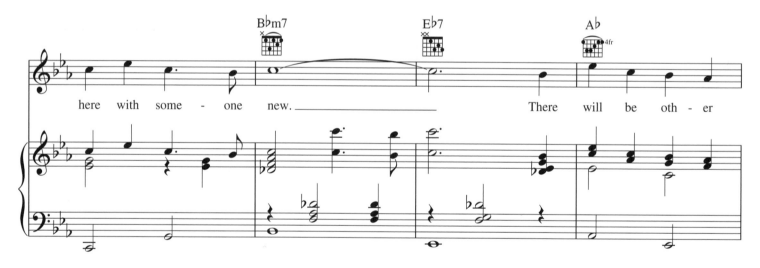

here with some - one new. _____ There will be oth - er

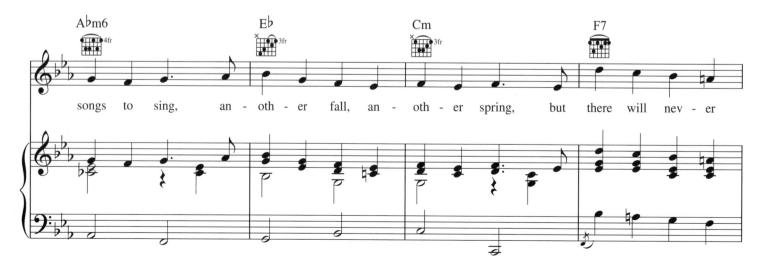

songs to sing, an - oth - er fall, an - oth - er spring, but there will nev - er

be an-oth-er you. _____ There will be oth-er lips that I may

kiss, _____ but they won't thrill me like yours used to do. _____

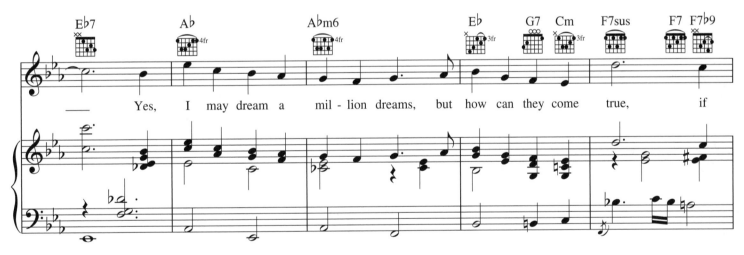

____ Yes, I may dream a mil-lion dreams, but how can they come true, if

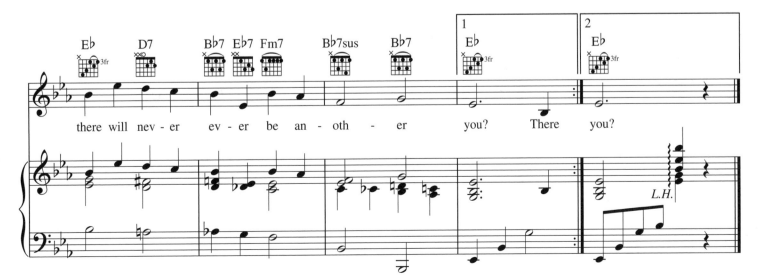

there will nev-er ev-er be an-oth-er you? There you?

THIS MASQUERADE

Words and Music by
LEON RUSSELL

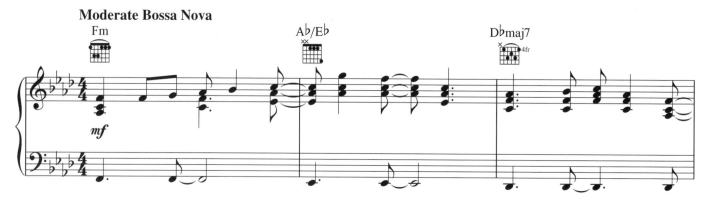

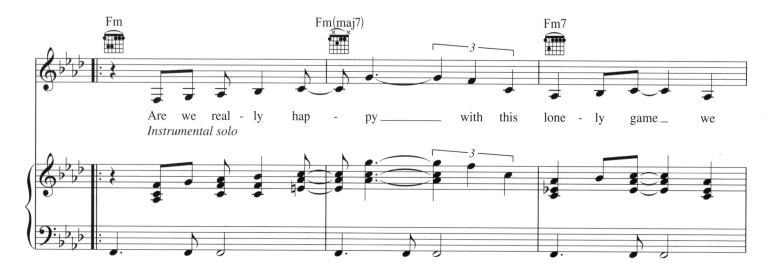

Are we real-ly hap-py ___ with this lone-ly game ___ we

Instrumental solo

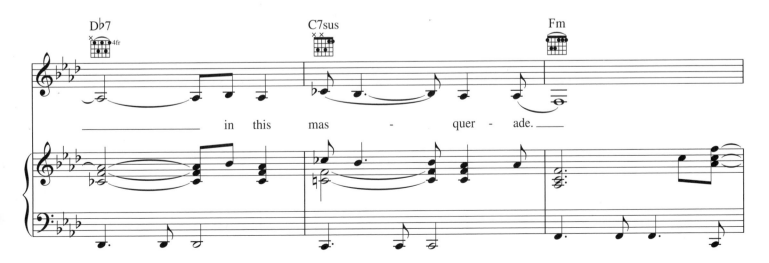

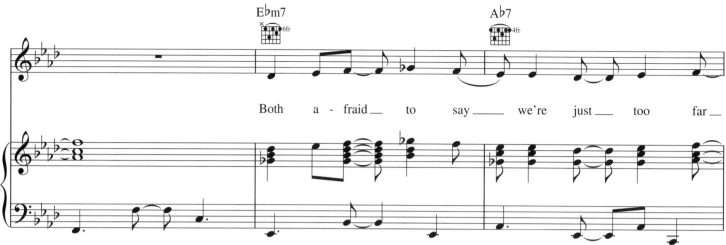

Both a-fraid to say we're just too far

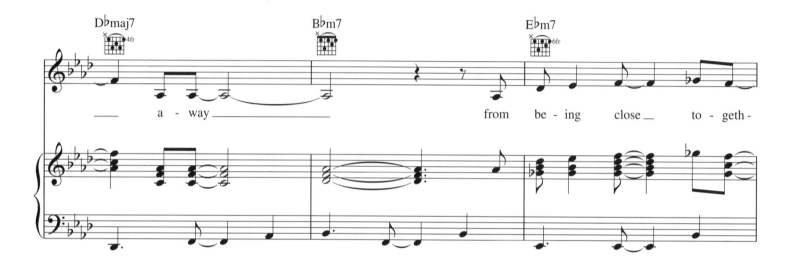

a-way from be-ing close to-geth-

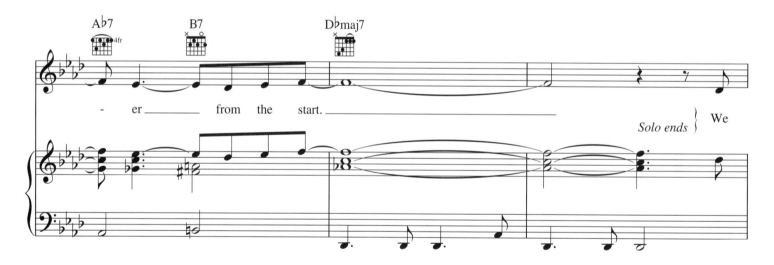

-er from the start.

Solo ends } We

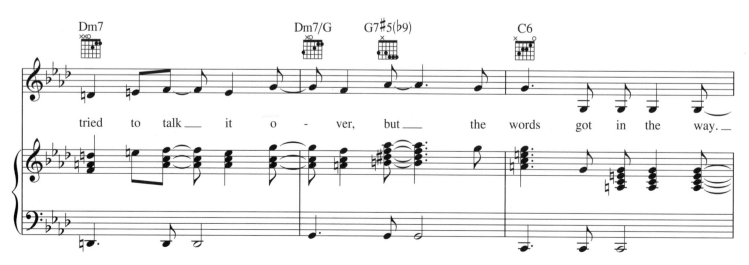

tried to talk it o-ver, but the words got in the way.

We're lost _____ in - side _____ this

lone - ly game ___ we play. ___ Thoughts of leav - ing dis -

- ap - pear ___ each ___ time ___ I see your eyes. ___

And no mat - ter how _____ hard I try _____ to

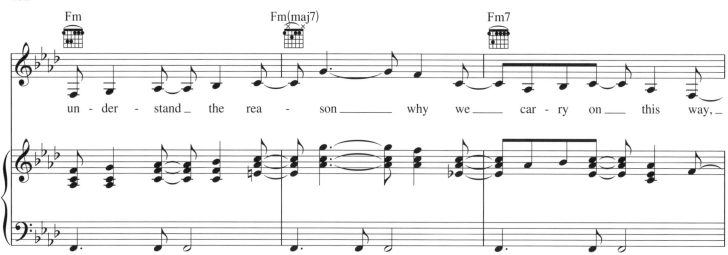

un - der - stand _ the rea - son _ why we _ car - ry on _ this way, _

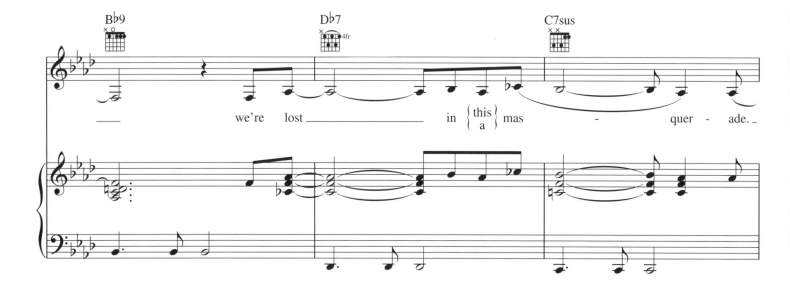

_ we're lost _ in {this / a} mas - quer - ade. _

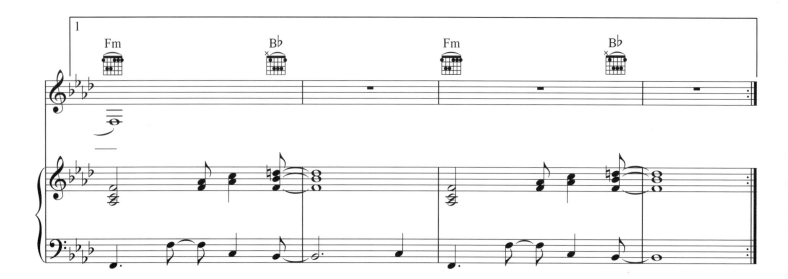

We're lost _____ in a mas - quer -

molto rit.

ade. _____

a tempo

Male: And we're lost _____ in a mas - quer - ade. _____

Repeat ad lib. and Fade | **Optional Ending**

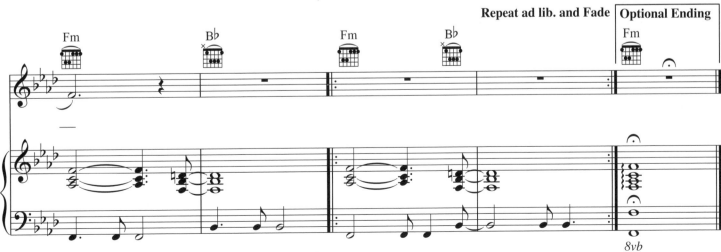

8vb

WALTZ FOR DEBBY

Lyric by GENE LEES
Music by BILL EVANS

THE WAY YOU LOOK TONIGHT

from SWING TIME

Words by DOROTHY FIELDS
Music by JEROME KERN

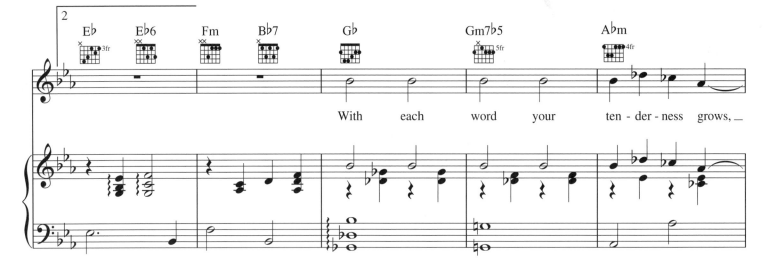

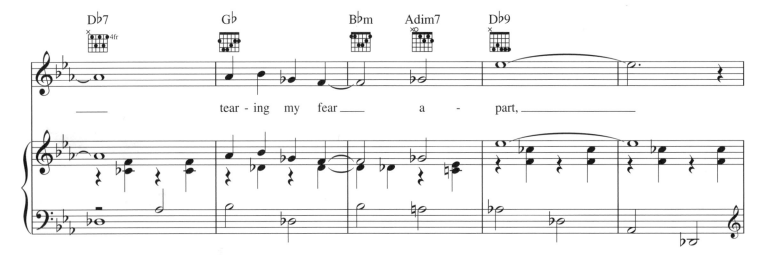

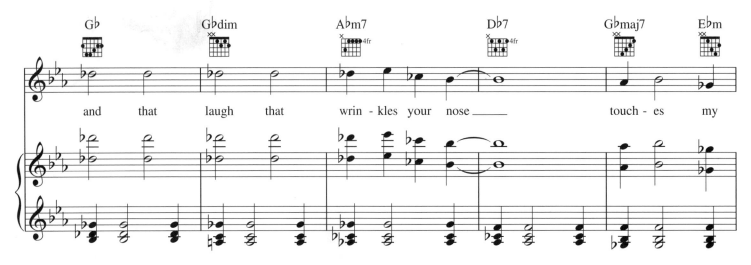

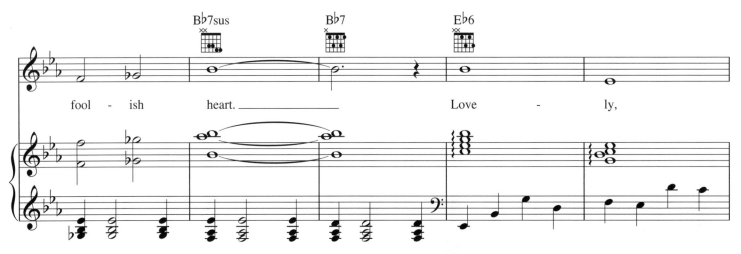

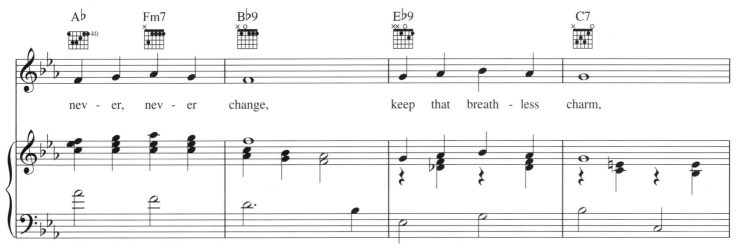

never, nev - er change, keep that breath - less charm,

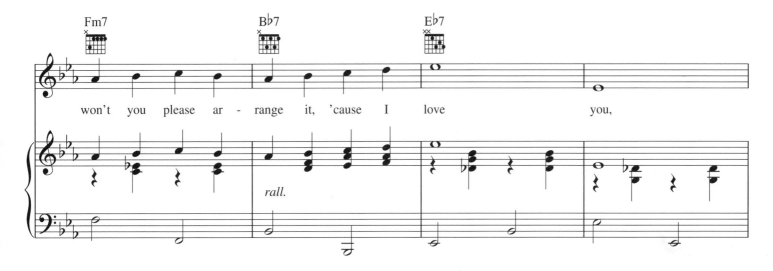

won't you please ar - range it, 'cause I love you, *rall.*

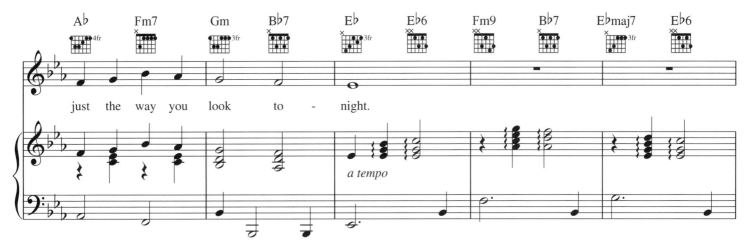

just the way you look to - night. *a tempo*

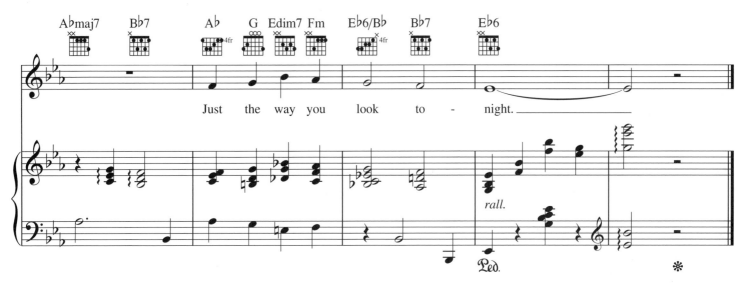

Just the way you look to - night. *rall.*

WHAT IS THIS THING CALLED LOVE?

from WAKE UP AND DREAM

Words and Music by
COLE PORTER

Moderately

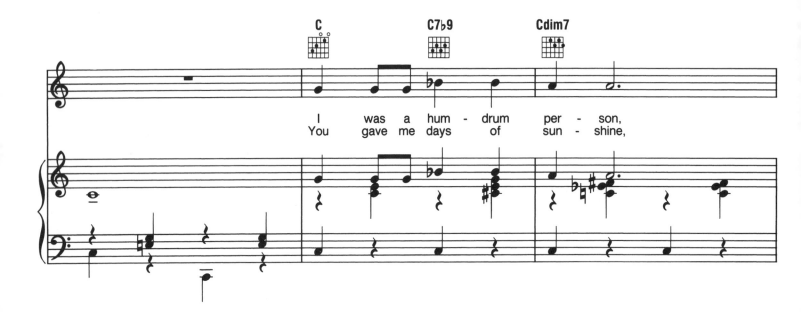

I was a hum - drum per - son,
You gave me days of sun - shine,

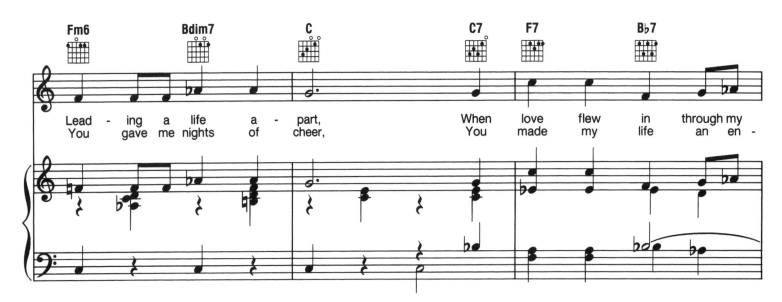

Lead - ing a life a - part,
You gave me nights of cheer,

When love flew in through my
You made my life an en -

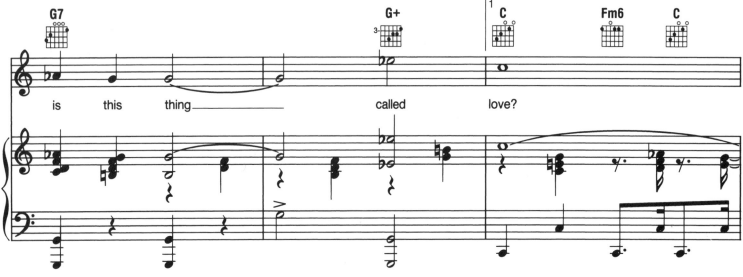

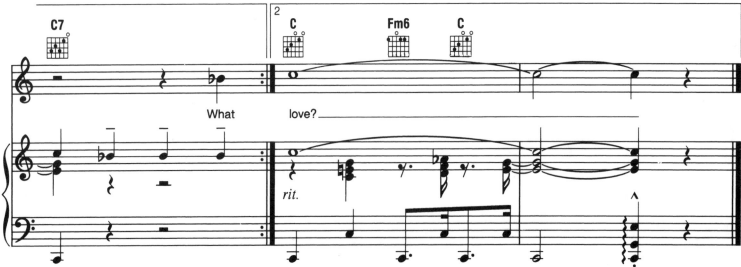

WHAT'S NEW?

Words by JOHNNY BURKE
Music by BOB HAGGART

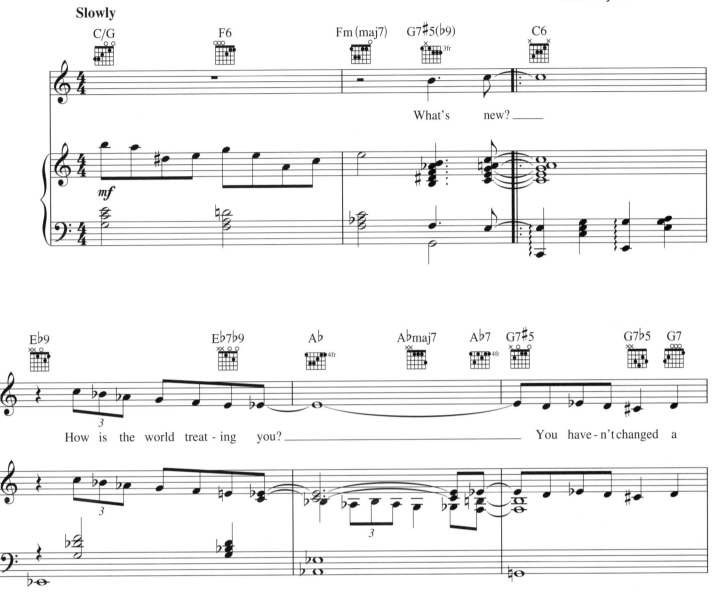

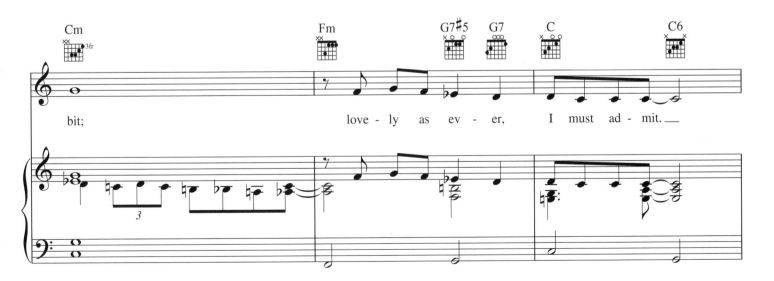

Lyrics:
What's new? ___
How is the world treat-ing you? ___ You have-n't changed a bit;
love-ly as ev-er, I must ad-mit. ___

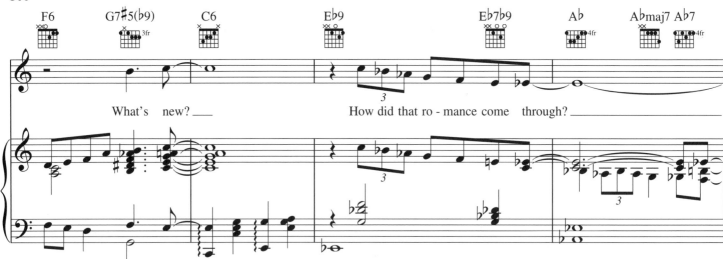

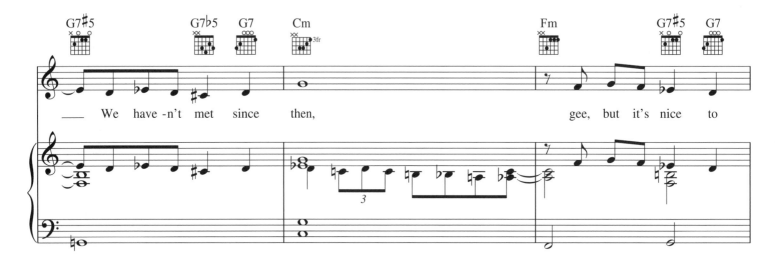

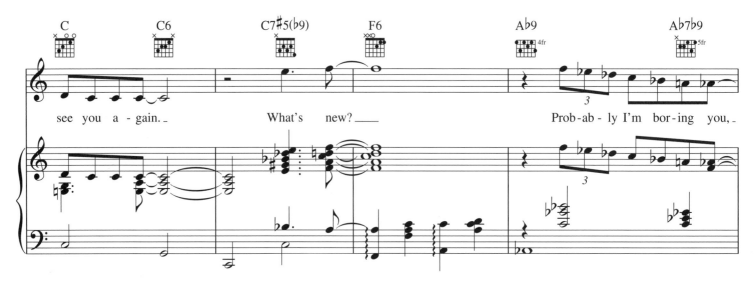

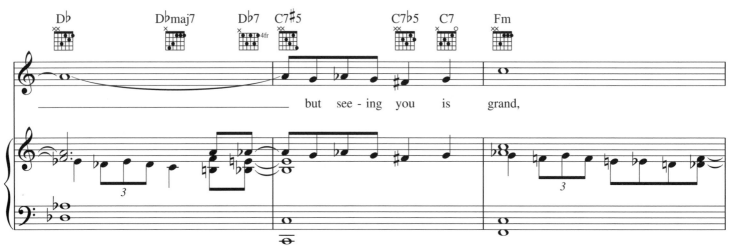

YESTERDAYS

from ROBERTA
from LOVELY TO LOOK AT

Words by OTTO HARBACH
Music by JEROME KERN

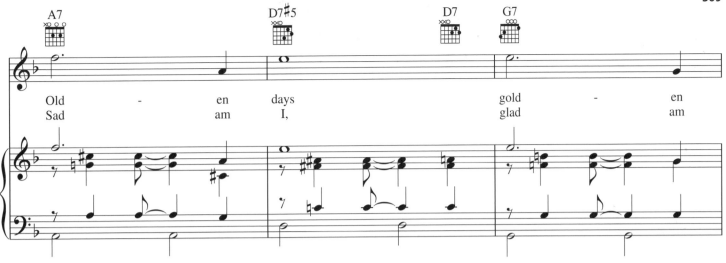

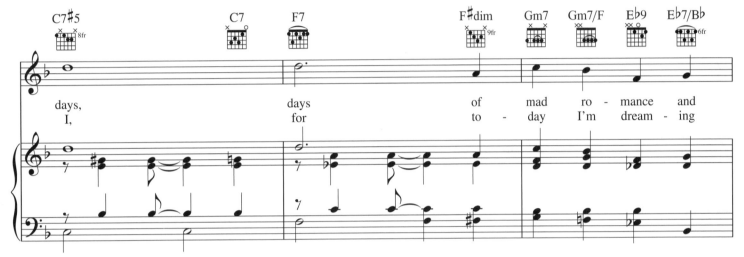

YOU ARE TOO BEAUTIFUL

from HALLELUJAH, I'M A BUM

Words by LORENZ HART
Music by RICHARD RODGERS

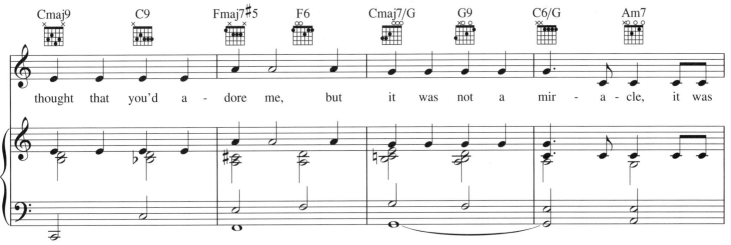

thought that you'd a - dore me, but it was not a mir - a - cle, it was

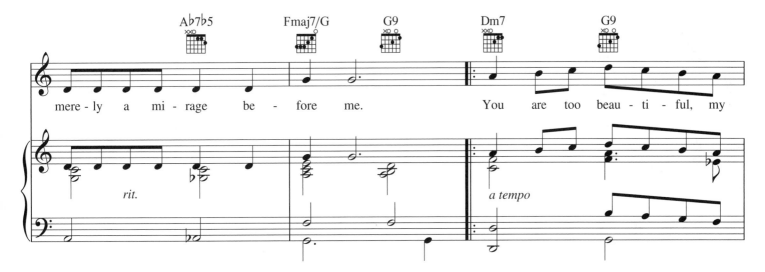

mere - ly a mi - rage be - fore me. You are too beau - ti - ful, my

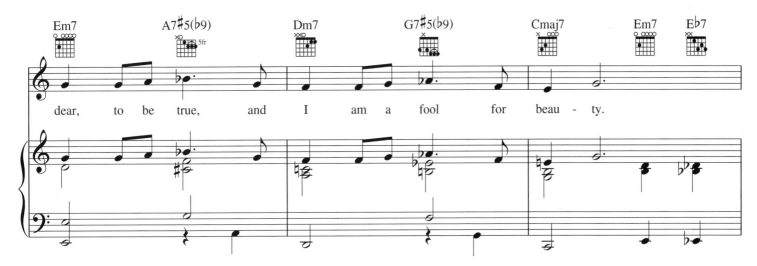

dear, to be true, and I am a fool for beau - ty.

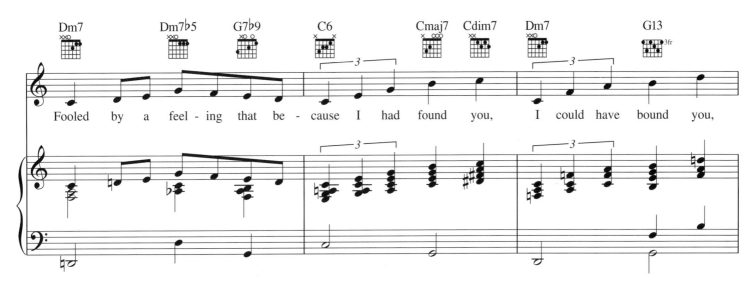

Fooled by a feel - ing that be - cause I had found you, I could have bound you,

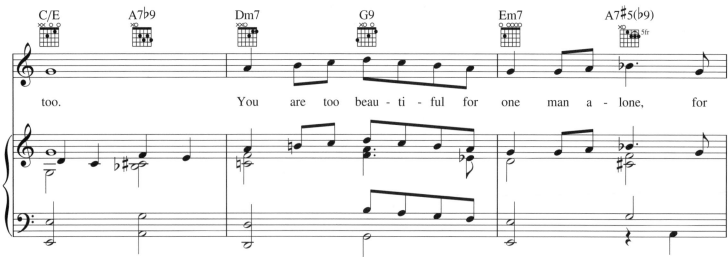

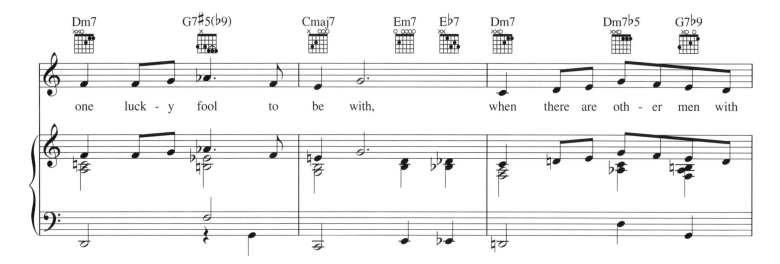

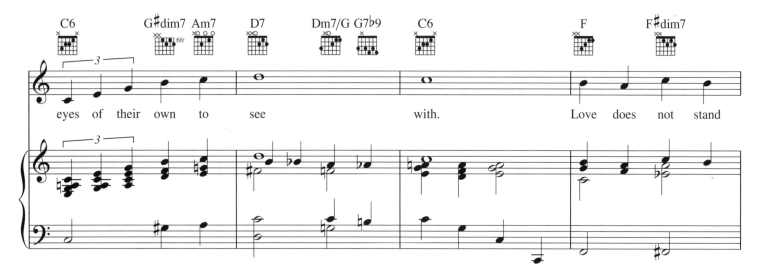

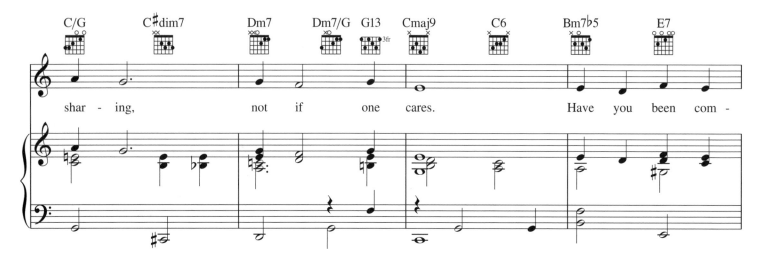

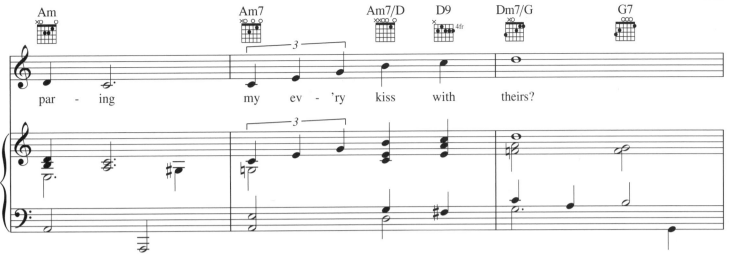

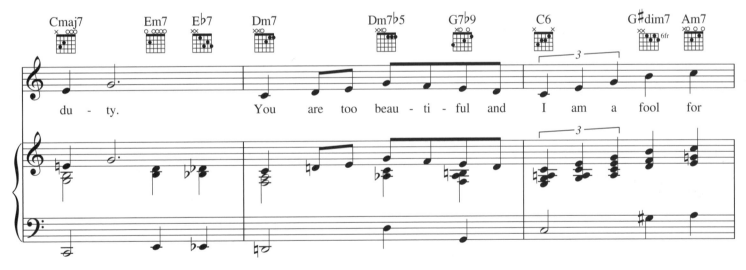

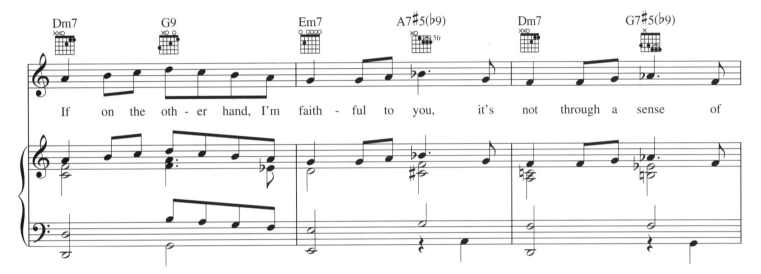

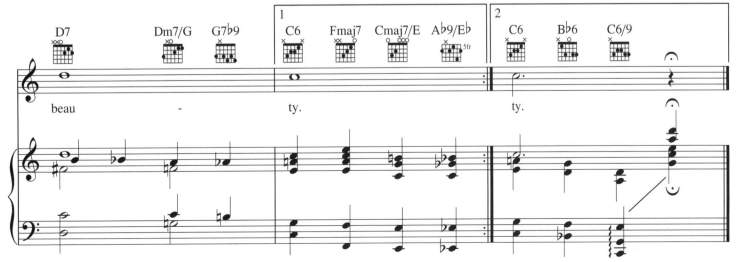

YOU DON'T KNOW WHAT LOVE IS

Words and Music by DON RAYE
and GENE DePAUL

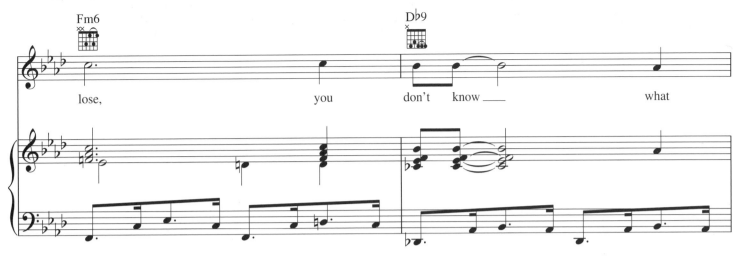

lose, you don't know ____ what

love is. ____ You don't know ____ how

lips hurt ____ un - til you've kissed and had to ____ pay the

cost; un - til you've flipped your heart and you have

lost, you don't know ___ what love is. ___ Do

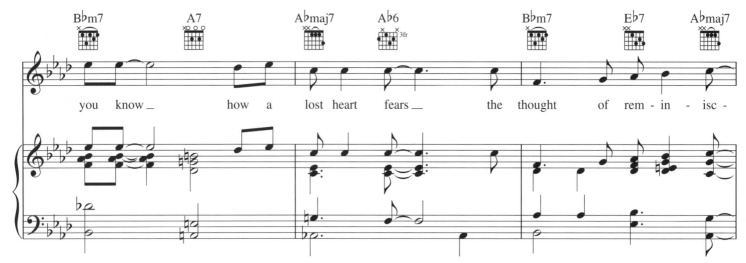

you know ___ how a lost heart fears ___ the thought of rem - in - isc -

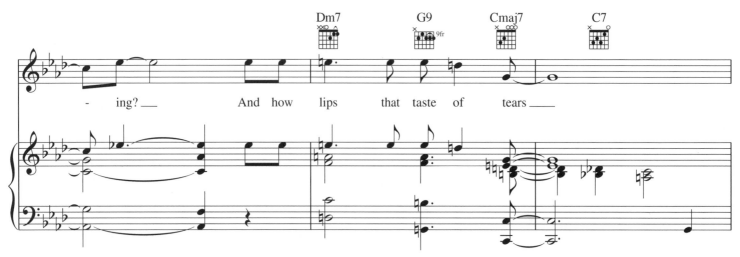

- ing? ___ And how lips that taste of tears ___

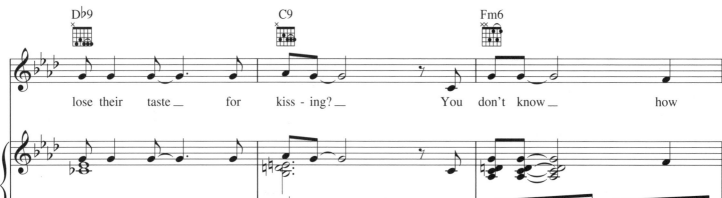

lose their taste ___ for kiss - ing? ___ You don't know ___ how

Big Books of Music

Our "Big Books" feature big selections of popular titles under one cover, perfect for performing musicians, music aficionados or the serious hobbyist. All books are arranged for piano, voice, and guitar, and feature stay-open binding, so the books lie flat without breaking the spine.

BIG BOOK OF BALLADS
63 songs.
00310485 ....$19.95

BIG BOOK OF BIG BAND HITS
84 songs.
00310701 ....$19.95

BIG BOOK OF BROADWAY
70 songs.
00311658 ....$19.95

BIG BOOK OF CHILDREN'S SONGS
55 songs.
00359261 ....$14.95

GREAT BIG BOOK OF CHILDREN'S SONGS
74 songs.
00310002 ....$14.95

FANTASTIC BIG BOOK OF CHILDREN'S SONGS
67 songs.
00311062 ....$16.95

MIGHTY BIG BOOK OF CHILDREN'S SONGS
65 songs.
00310467 ....$14.95

REALLY BIG BOOK OF CHILDREN'S SONGS
63 songs.
00310372 ....$15.95

BIG BOOK OF CHILDREN'S MOVIE SONGS
66 songs.
00310731 ....$17.95

BIG BOOK OF CHRISTMAS SONGS
126 songs.
00311520 ....$19.95

BIG BOOK OF CLASSIC ROCK
77 songs.
00310801 ....$19.95

BIG BOOK OF CLASSICAL MUSIC
100 songs.
00310508 ....$19.95

BIG BOOK OF CONTEMPORARY CHRISTIAN FAVORITES
50 songs.
00310021 ....$19.95

BIG BOOK OF COUNTRY MUSIC
63 songs.
00310188 ....$19.95

BIG BOOK OF DISCO & FUNK
70 songs.
00310878 ....$19.95

BIG BOOK OF EARLY ROCK N' ROLL
99 songs.
00310398 ....$19.95

BIG BOOK OF FOLK POP ROCK
80 songs.
00311125 ....$19.95

BIG BOOK OF GOSPEL SONGS
100 songs.
00310604 ....$19.95

BIG BOOK OF HYMNS
125 hymns.
00310510 ....$17.95

BIG BOOK OF IRISH SONGS
76 songs.
00310981 ....$16.95

BIG BOOK OF JAZZ
75 songs.
00311557 ....$19.95

BIG BOOK OF LATIN AMERICAN SONGS
89 songs.
00311562 ....$19.95

BIG BOOK OF LOVE SONGS
80 songs.
00310784 ....$19.95

BIG BOOK OF MOTOWN
84 songs.
00311061 ....$19.95

BIG BOOK OF MOVIE MUSIC
72 songs.
00311582 ....$19.95

BIG BOOK OF NOSTALGIA
160 songs.
00310004 ....$19.95

BIG BOOK OF OLDIES
73 songs.
00310756 ....$19.95

BIG BOOK OF RHYTHM & BLUES
67 songs.
00310169 ....$19.95

BIG BOOK OF ROCK
78 songs.
00311566 ....$19.95

BIG BOOK OF SOUL
71 songs.
00310771 ....$19.95

BIG BOOK OF STANDARDS
86 songs.
00311667 ....$19.95

BIG BOOK OF SWING
84 songs.
00310359 ....$19.95

BIG BOOK OF TORCH SONGS
75 songs.
00310561 ....$19.95

BIG BOOK OF TV THEME SONGS
78 songs.
00310504 ....$19.95

BIG BOOK OF WEDDING MUSIC
77 songs.
00311567 ....$19.95

FOR MORE INFORMATION, SEE YOUR LOCAL MUSIC DEALER,
OR WRITE TO:

HAL•LEONARD® CORPORATION

7777 W. BLUEMOUND RD. P.O. BOX 13819 MILWAUKEE, WI 53213

Prices, contents, and availability subject to change without notice.

Visit **www.halleonard.com**
for our entire catalog and to view our complete songlists.

0105

THE BEST EVER COLLECTION

ARRANGED FOR PIANO, VOICE AND GUITAR

150 of the Most Beautiful Songs Ever
150 ballads: Bewitched • (They Long to Be) Close to You • How Deep Is Your Love • I'll Be Seeing You • Unchained Melody • Yesterday • Young at Heart • more.
00360735...$24.95

Best Acoustic Rock Songs Ever
65 acoustic hits: Dust in the Wind • Fast Car • I Will Remember You • Landslide • Leaving on a Jet Plane • Maggie May • Tears in Heaven • Yesterday • more.
00310984...$19.95

Best Big Band Songs Ever
Over 60 big band hits: Boogie Woogie Bugle Boy • Don't Get Around Much Anymore • In the Mood • Moonglow • Sentimental Journey • Who's Sorry Now • more.
00359129...$16.95

Best Broadway Songs Ever
Over 70 songs in all! Includes: All I Ask of You • Bess, You Is My Woman • Climb Ev'ry Mountain • Comedy Tonight • If I Were a Rich Man • Ol' Man River • more!
00309155...$22.95

Best Children's Songs Ever
Over 100 songs: Bingo • Eensy Weensy Spider • The Farmer in the Dell • On Top of Spaghetti • Puff the Magic Dragon • Twinkle, Twinkle Little Star • and more.
00310360 (Easy Piano)......................................$19.95

Best Christmas Songs Ever
More than 60 holiday favorites: Frosty the Snow Man • A Holly Jolly Christmas • I'll Be Home for Christmas • Rudolph, The Red-Nosed Reindeer • Silver Bells • more.
00359130...$19.95

Best Classic Rock Songs Ever
Over 60 hits: American Woman • Bang a Gong • Cold As Ice • Heartache Tonight • Rock and Roll All Nite • Smoke on the Water • Wonderful Tonight • and more.
00310800...$18.95

Best Classical Songs Ever
Over 80 of classical favorites: Ave Maria • Canon in D • Eine Kleine Nachtmusik • Für Elise • Lacrymosa • Ode to Joy • William Tell Overture • and many more.
00310674 (Piano Solo).....................................$19.95

Best Contemporary Christian Songs Ever
Over 70 favorites, including: Awesome God • El Shaddai • Friends • Jesus Freak • People Need the Lord • Place in This World • Serve the Lord • Thy Word • more.
00310558...$19.95

Best Country Songs Ever
78 classic country hits: Always on My Mind • Crazy • Daddy Sang Bass • Forever and Ever, Amen • God Bless the U.S.A. • I Fall to Pieces • Through the Years • more.
00359135...$17.95

Best Early Rock 'n' Roll Songs Ever
Over 70 songs, including: Book of Love • Crying • Do Wah Diddy Diddy • Louie, Louie • Peggy Sue • Shout • Splish Splash • Stand By Me • Tequila • and more.
00310816...$17.95

Best Easy Listening Songs Ever
75 mellow favorites: (They Long to Be) Close to You • Every Breath You Take • How Am I Supposed to Live Without You • Unchained Melody • more.
00359193...$18.95

Best Gospel Songs Ever
80 gospel songs: Amazing Grace • Daddy Sang Bass • How Great Thou Art • I'll Fly Away • Just a Closer Walk with Thee • The Old Rugged Cross • more.
00310503...$19.95

Best Hymns Ever
118 hymns: Abide with Me • Every Time I Feel the Spirit • He Leadeth Me • I Love to Tell the Story • Were You There? • When I Survey the Wondrous Cross • and more.
00310774...$17.95

Best Jazz Standards Ever
77 jazz hits: April in Paris • Beyond the Sea • Don't Get Around Much Anymore • Misty • Satin Doll • So Nice (Summer Samba) • Unforgettable • and more.
00311641...$19.95

More of the Best Jazz Standards Ever
74 beloved jazz hits: Ain't Misbehavin' • Blue Skies • Come Fly with Me • Honeysuckle Rose • The Lady Is a Tramp • Moon River • My Funny Valentine • and more.
00311023...$19.95

Best Latin Songs Ever
67 songs: Besame Mucho (Kiss Me Much) • The Girl from Ipanema • Malaguena • Slightly Out of Tune (Desafinado) • Summer Samba (So Nice) • and more.
00310355...$19.95

Best Love Songs Ever
65 favorite love songs, including: Endless Love • Here and Now • Love Takes Time • Misty • My Funny Valentine • So in Love • You Needed Me • Your Song.
00359198...$19.95

Best Movie Songs Ever
74 songs from the movies: Almost Paradise • Chariots of Fire • My Heart Will Go On • Take My Breath Away • Unchained Melody • You'll Be in My Heart • more.
00310063...$19.95

Best Praise & Worship Songs Ever
80 all-time favorites: Awesome God • Breathe • Here I Am to Worship • I Could Sing of Your Love Forever • Open the Eyes of My Heart • Shout to the Lord • more.
00310063...$19.95

Best R&B Songs Ever
66 songs, including: Baby Love • Endless Love • Here and Now • I Will Survive • Saving All My Love for You • Stand By Me • What's Going On • and more.
00310184...$19.95

Best Rock Songs Ever
Over 60 songs: All Shook Up • Blue Suede Shoes • Born to Be Wild • Every Breath You Take • Free Bird • Hey Jude • We Got the Beat • Wild Thing • more!
00490424...$18.95

Best Songs Ever
Over 70 must-own classics: Edelweiss • Love Me Tender • Memory • My Funny Valentine • Tears in Heaven • Unforgettable • A Whole New World • and more.
00359224...$22.95

More of the Best Songs Ever
79 more favorites: April in Paris • Candle in the Wind • Endless Love • Misty • My Blue Heaven • My Heart Will Go On • Stella by Starlight • Witchcraft • more.
00310437...$19.95

Best Standards Ever, Vol. 1 (A-L)
72 beautiful ballads, including: All the Things You Are • Bewitched • God Bless' the Child • I've Got You Under My Skin • The Lady Is a Tramp • more.
00359231...$16.95

More of the Best Standards Ever, Vol. 1 (A-L)
76 all-time favorites: Ain't Misbehavin' • Always • Autumn in New York • Desafinado • Fever • Fly Me to the Moon • Georgia on My Mind • and more.
00310813...$17.95

Best Standards Ever, Vol. 2 (M-Z)
72 songs: Makin' Whoopee • Misty • My Funny Valentine • People Will Say We're in Love • Smoke Gets in Your Eyes • Strangers in the Night • Tuxedo Junction • more.
00359232...$16.95

More of the Best Standards Ever, Vol. 2 (M-Z)
75 more stunning standards: Mona Lisa • Mood Indigo • Moon River • Norwegian Wood • Route 66 • Sentimental Journey • Stella by Starlight • What'll I Do? • and more.
00310814...$17.95

Best Torch Songs Ever
70 sad and sultry favorites: All by Myself • Crazy • Fever • I Will Remember You • Misty • Stormy Weather (Keeps Rainin' All the Time) • Unchained Melody • and more.
00311027...$19.95

Best TV Songs Ever
Over 50 fun and catchy theme songs: The Addams Family • The Brady Bunch • Happy Days • Mission: Impossible • Where Everybody Knows Your Name • and more!
00311048...$17.95

Best Wedding Songs Ever
70 songs of love and commitment: All I Ask of You • Endless Love • The Lord's Prayer • My Heart Will Go On • Trumpet Voluntary • Wedding March • and more.
00311096...$17.95

FOR MORE INFORMATION, SEE YOUR LOCAL MUSIC DEALER, OR WRITE TO:

HAL•LEONARD® CORPORATION
7777 W. BLUEMOUND RD. P.O. BOX 13819 MILWAUKEE, WI 53213

Visit us on-line for complete songlists at
www.halleonard.com

Prices, contents and availability subject to change without notice. Not all products available outside the U.S.A.

0205

Classic Collections Of Your Favorite Songs

arranged for piano, voice, and guitar.

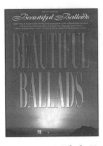

Beautiful Ballads

A massive collection of 87 songs, including: April in Paris • Autumn in New York • Call Me Irresponsible • Cry Me a River • I Wish You Love • I'll Be Seeing You • If • Imagine • Isn't It Romantic? • It's Impossible (Somos Novios) • Mona Lisa • Moon River • People • The Way We Were • A Whole New World (Aladdin's Theme) • and more.
00311679 ....$17.95

Irving Berlin Anthology

A comprehensive collection of 61 timeless songs with a bio, song background notes, and photos. Songs include: Always • Blue Skies • Cheek to Cheek • God Bless America • Marie • Puttin' on the Ritz • Steppin' Out with My Baby • There's No Business Like Show Business • White Christmas • (I Wonder Why?) You're Just in Love • and more.
00312493 ....$22.95

The Big Book of Standards

86 classics essential to any music library, including: April in Paris • Autumn in New York • Blue Skies • Cheek to Cheek • Heart and Soul • I Left My Heart in San Francisco • In the Mood • Isn't It Romantic? • Mona Lisa • Moon River • The Nearness of You • Out of Nowhere • Spanish Eyes • Star Dust • Stella by Starlight • That Old Black Magic • They Say It's Wonderful • What Now My Love • and more.
00311667 ....$19.95

Broadway Deluxe

This exciting collection of 125 of Broadway's biggest show tunes is deluxe indeed! Includes such showstoppers as: Bewitched • Cabaret • Camelot • Day by Day • Hello Young Lovers • I Could Have Danced All Night • I've Grown Accustomed to Her Face • If Ever I Would Leave You • The Lady Is a Tramp • I Talk to the Trees • My Heart Belongs to Daddy • Oklahoma • September Song • Seventy Six Trombones • Try to Remember • and more!
00309245 ....$24.95

Classic Jazz Standards

56 jazz essentials: All the Things You Are • Don't Get Around Much Anymore • How Deep Is the Ocean • In the Wee Small Hours of the Morning • Polka Dots and Moonbeams • Satin Doll • Skylark • Tangerine • Tenderly • What's New? • and more.
00310310 ....$16.95

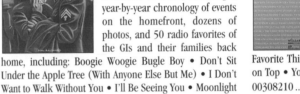

I'll Be Seeing You: 50 Songs of World War II

A salute to the music and memories of WWII, including a year-by-year chronology of events on the homefront, dozens of photos, and 50 radio favorites of the GIs and their families back home, including: Boogie Woogie Bugle Boy • Don't Sit Under the Apple Tree (With Anyone Else But Me) • I Don't Want to Walk Without You • I'll Be Seeing You • Moonlight in Vermont • There's a Star-Spangled Banner Waving Somewhere • You'd Be So Nice to Come Home To • and more.
00311698 ....$19.95

Lounge Music

Features 45 top requests of the martini crowd: Alfie • Beyond the Sea • Blue Velvet • Call Me Irresponsible • Copacabana • Danke Schoen • Feelings • The Girl from Ipanema • I Will Survive • Mandy • Misty • More • People • That's Life • more.
00310193 ....$14.95

Best of Cole Porter

38 of his classics, including: All of You • Anything Goes • Be a Clown • Don't Fence Me In • I Get a Kick Out of You • In the Still of the Night • Let's Do It (Let's Fall in Love) • Night and Day • You Do Something to Me • and many more.
00311577 ....$14.95

Big Band Favorites

A great collection of 70 of the best Swing Era songs, including: East of the Sun • Honeysuckle Rose • I Can't Get Started with You • I'll Be Seeing You • In the Mood • Let's Get Away from It All • Moonglow • Moonlight in Vermont • Opus One • Stompin' at the Savoy • Tuxedo Junction • more!
00310445 ....$16.95

The Best of Rodgers & Hammerstein

A capsule of 26 classics from this legendary duo. Songs include: Climb Ev'ry Mountain • Edelweiss • Getting to Know You • I'm Gonna Wash That Man Right Outta My Hair • My Favorite Things • Oklahoma • The Surrey with the Fringe on Top • You'll Never Walk Alone • and more.
00308210 ....$16.95

The Best Songs Ever – 5th Edition

Over 70 must-own classics, including: All I Ask of You • Body and Soul • Crazy • Fly Me to the Moon • Here's That Rainy Day • Imagine • Love Me Tender • Memory • Moonlight in Vermont • My Funny Valentine • People • Satin Doll • Save the Best for Last • Tears in Heaven • A Time for Us • The Way We Were • What a Wonderful World • When I Fall in Love • and more.
00359224 ....$22.95

Torch Songs

Sing your heart out with this collection of 59 sultry jazz and big band melancholy masterpieces, including: Angel Eyes • Cry Me a River • I Can't Get Started • I Got It Bad and That Ain't Good • I'm Glad There Is You • Lover Man (Oh, Where Can You Be?) • Misty • My Funny Valentine • Stormy Weather • and many more! 224 pages.
00490446 ....$17.95